Becoming
A Corporate
Art Consultant

The Handbook for Corporate Art Consultation

Barbara Markoff

First Paperback Printing 2009

Copyright © 2009 by PFM Books, a Division of PFM Seminars & Barbara Markoff

ISBN: 978-0-9663189-6-8

Library of Congress Control Number: 2009913226

Barbara Markoff
Corporate Art Consultant
Artrageous!
5350-A Eastgate Mall, San Diego, CA   92121
858-452-7280 (work) • 858-452-7210 (fax) • barbara@theartconsultant.biz

Limits of Liability

The author and publisher will not be held liable for your misuse of this material.
This book is strictly for informational and educational purposes.

Disclaimer

The purpose of this book is to educate and empower. The author and/ or publisher do not guarantee that anyone following these techniques, suggestions, tips, ideas, or strategies will become successful. The author and/or publisher shall have neither liability nor responsibility to anyone with respect to any loss or damage caused, or alleged to be caused, directly or indirectly by the information contained in this book.

Manufactured in China

CONTENTS

Introduction

Why write a book on corporate art consultation? I have been working as an art consultant in the art and framing industry for almost 30 years, and there is very little reference material available on the subject of corporate art consultation. If I had found a book along the way to guide me through the process of becoming an art consultant, life would have been much easier. A comprehensive and practical handbook did not exist. Let me clarify that I do not sell investment artwork. I design and sell art programs to corporate clients to enhance their work environments. The majority of budgets I propose are anywhere from $5,000 to $200,000. The skills I have honed will help my readers work in this budget range. Of course larger budget jobs exist but less frequently. In order to gain the expertise to pursue larger jobs, it is important to learn the basics of corporate art consultation. I sell art, framing, and all of the other services needed for a corporate art program. Corporate clients are looking for artwork to solidify their corporate identity, and this book will help you understand how that is accomplished.

I learned by trial and error and figured out the most successful strategies by relying on my own intuition. Growing up in a family business and having all of my siblings as entrepreneurs gave me a built-in support system. Early on in my career I had learned the basic business practices of integrity, value, honesty, ethics, and customer service from my father, Max Greenberg, co-founder of Tennessee Mat Company, a manufacturing company of industrial matting. Being an entrepreneur was in my blood. Since 1981 I have worked alongside my husband, Rob Markoff, running a successful art and framing business in San Diego called Artrageous!

I wrote this book to help artists, art consultants, gallery owners, frame shop owners, interior designers, and other design professionals understand corporate art consultation. It is a niche I have carved out for myself and one I am passionate about. Realizing that I could grow our business by providing art consultation services to corporate clients, I focused my energies in the direction of working outside of our retail showroom. I joined networking groups and constantly added new business contacts. I learned that making business friends and sharing business information was vital to my success. Adding new artists was also part of the process and remains a top priority for me. I learned how to find and meet with decision makers, how to read and review blueprints and floor plans, how to make presentations, how to write proposals, how to place and install artwork, and much more.

To share my experiences I wrote articles on art consultation and began a series of seminars to educate design professionals about what the profession is all about. I mentored individuals who had taken my classes and needed further direction. All of these activities led up to writing this book so I could help others understand the process.

What qualifies me to be an art consultant? I have an undergraduate degree in fine art and a master's degree in art therapy. I draw upon my knowledge of fine art, art history, art therapy, picture framing, and business experience of over 28 years. In the process of becoming an art consultant I wore many hats. Being an art consultant is like being part art educator, part art historian, part designer, part rainmaker, part psychologist, part sales person, part investigator, and part business friend. In addition to educating clients about art and design,

I keep a positive attitude and aggressively go after business.

Becoming an art consultant has been a fun and interesting journey. I have made many wonderful friends along the way, and I receive tremendous pleasure from the positive feedback I get from clients pleased with their art programs. In order to achieve success it takes a driven, optimistic individual with a background in art and framing. It is not a profession for the person easily discouraged or unwilling to take risks. It takes dedication and perseverance. I hope this book will ease the path a bit and navigate you through many successful projects.

Chapter 1

What is a Corporate Art Consultant?

Acorporate art consultant uses his/her expertise drawing upon a body of knowledge including framing design, art history, art printing methods, and art resources to guide clients through the process of selecting an art program. Like interior designers, art consultants may specialize in corporate, residential design, or both. I am often asked why I prefer working with corporate rather than retail clients. The answer involves time lines, larger budgets, and most importantly creative control over a sizable project. I welcome the opportunity to interact with corporate clients who are decisive, receptive, and willing to turn the art program over to me, relying on my expertise and trained eye. Conversely, retail art consultation moves slower and sales are usually dependent upon family members making decisions and spending household money together. While many corporate jobs must be completed for a pending opening of the building or offices, residential clients do not have a sense of urgency to complete their projects.

Art consultants combine many talents and often feel like they are playing the roles of psychologist, designer, art educator, sales person, investigator, and business friend. It is all about building relationships with business people who need personalized service. In the corporate setting, the art consultant is most often driving the sale of the artwork and the framing within the parameters of the job. Vision is the vital ingredient the art consultant brings to the table. The passion for art and framing combine with business savvy as the consultant transforms an empty, stark office into a finished, flowing, and well integrated space reflecting the corporate image, culture, and attitude of the occupants. In addition to possessing a certain skill level, art consultants must work in a metropolitan area where the demographics can support their business. Realistically it would be difficult to succeed as an art consultant where the population is under 50,000. The larger the city the more opportunity there is for art placement.

In many situations, art consultants are part of a team of professionals including project managers, interior designers, facilities managers, architects, and corporate executives. Each team member has his/her own specific expertise to bring to the project. All team members coordinate their efforts and meet regularly to discuss the progress of the project. Art consultants are expected to read and understand blueprints, prepare budgets, specify artwork, make art presentations, prepare and revise proposals, facilitate commissions, design and coordinate picture framing, oversee art placement, and direct installations. Scheduled jobs will overlap, and it is not uncommon for an art consultant to be working on many jobs at different phases simultaneously. In addition to overseeing these jobs, the consultant must be prepared to have the financial capacity to carry receivables. A good banking relationship needs to be in place with a reasonable line of credit. Purchase orders do not pay the bills. It could take 90 days to 6 months to get paid on some large projects.

Networking plays a large part in landing corporate jobs. I will discuss this later in the book, but I cannot stress enough the importance of sharing information with other business people. Be involved in your community and network extensively. Art consultants need to spread the word through the business community, and what better way to gain exposure than through networking with other high-level business people.

Art consultants are called upon to diagnose a variety of situations and recommend solutions. It is not simply dropping off art catalogs and having clients select artwork. Decision makers look to consultants for expert advice and recommendations. Sometimes the artwork specified will be selected to blend with the interior design. Other times the art program will involve framing historical photographs and memorabilia owned by the company. With healthcare facilities, the artwork will need to be sensitive and calming. The art procurement process varies considerably from one job to the next. Since the art consultant is hired as the expert, he/she is expected to listen to the client and determine the most suitable artwork based on budget considerations. It is a service-oriented profession.

Our company sells both art and framing, and since we do our own framing I have full control over turnaround times, materials, and craftsmanship. If you do not offer framing as part of your business, you will need to form a close relationship with a contract framer you can rely on. All picture framing is not the same. You will need to educate yourself about matting materials, glazing products, archival treatments, framing design that is not only good looking but functional, and types of frames available in the marketplace. In addition, you will need to know how and when to specify the most appropriate and cost effective framing materials.

Working within a budget is an acquired skill. Your client may have unrealistic expectations when it comes to what framing materials cost, and you will be put into a position of justifying your prices. Balancing excellent framing design with cost effective materials will not always be easy, but the more time you invest in learning about framing, the easier it will be for you to educate your client and close sales.

In summary an art consultant is:

1. Part psychologist, part designer, part art educator, part sales person, part investigator, and part business friend.
2. An educated professional with a working knowledge of art, art history, print making, and framing design.
3. Part of a design team with interior designers, architects, project managers, facilities managers, and corporate executives.
4. A motivated networking member eagerly gathering and sharing information.
5. A confident problem solver and good listener.
6. An experienced professional who guides the client through each phase of the process.
7. An expert who will diagnose and recommend.
8. A seasoned professional who specifies public art for a work environment or institutional setting.
9. A sales representative who educates the client about the most appropriate and cost-effective framing materials.

Who is the corporate client?

Corporations or companies are comprised of groups of people working in some hierarchy all with a common company culture. Despite being well educated, a typical corporate representative often feels intimidated when choosing fine art and looks for a professional consultant to handle this daunting task. Not only may corporate clients feel out of their comfort zone, but most likely they are also quite busy maintaining their regular business schedule with little time to devote to an art program. Time is a very precious commodity for corporate executives. Consequently, they are looking for a confident, experienced professional to turn over the task of providing an inspiring, fresh, and aesthetically pleasing art plan that will blend with their furniture and interior décor. Corporate clients want art consultants who understand their needs and can solve problems.

The key to success is understanding the needs of the client, listening to them, and demonstrating expertise. People in business will choose an art consultant based on the consultant's confidence level and ability to deliver. Each job has a separate set of circumstances. By exuding confidence and enthusiasm and educating clients about the benefits of the art program, clients will feel relieved to turn over the project to a professional. Busy clients will know the job will be done right and hassle free for them.

The consultant's job is to educate the client about how the artwork will achieve the aesthetic goals and functions he/she is looking for. Before any problem solving can begin, the consultant must ask critical questions to learn as much as possible about the client's business. In anticipation of the first meeting, check the company's website and do the necessary research to find out what the company is all about.

Key questions and important information you need to find out:
1. What does the business do? If it manufactures a product, what is the product?
2. How long has the company been in business?
3. How large is the company? How many employees does it have?
4. Do they have other locations? If so, how many and where are they located?
5. Who visits the business and how regularly?
6. Are there any expansion plans?
7. Who are the executives? Get their names and positions.

Equally important, the consultant needs to know why the business wants to purchase artwork. Negotiations often center around why artwork is purchased and how the corporate look will be reinforced by the artwork to achieve these goals.

Businesses generally purchase artwork for one or more of the following reasons:
1. To project a professional image for customers, suppliers, bankers, etc.
2. To soothe, comfort, and welcome visitors.
3. To enhance employee morale.
4. To market or promote their business products.
5. To add visual interest to bare walls and add to the overall ambiance of the environment.
6. To promote local artists in the community.
7. To help define corporate identity and branding.

Art budgets vary depending on the size of the company, the size of the occupied space, and the company's needs at a given time. As a corporate art consultant, evaluate your skills and decide where to best focus your energy. Determine what kinds of artwork you feel knowledgeable enough to sell. A novice consultant may begin with selling posters and giclees for several years before moving into selling paintings and commissioned artwork. Know your comfort level and sell with confidence. A corporation may have a $90,000 budget for placing a sculpture in the lobby, but are you knowledgeable enough to handle this kind of sale? If you are in over your head, it is best to politely decline the opportunity or refer another consultant.

My business philosophy is, *Go after the business; do not expect it to come to you.* Part of being an art consultant is having the mindset and motivation to constantly find and cultivate new clients and build relationships. It is all about building and maintaining relationships with business people who need personalized service and an expert to help them with art and framing projects. We all know business people like to do business with friends, and you can never have enough business friends. Art consultants should be positioning themselves to make new business contacts every day. These contacts lead to more business.

What does an art consultant do?
1. Presents art and framing program to client.
2. Maintains working relationships with artists.
3. Takes charge of art procurement.
4. Adds new artists regularly.
5. Prepares an art budget.
6. Understands blueprints and floor plans.
7. Diagnoses the situation and makes recommendations.
8. Educates the client about the functions of artwork.
9. Advises the client about the types of artwork available and its appropriateness.
10. Maintains business relationships.
11. Networks to build new relationships.
12. Presents a professional image and keeps a positive outlook.
13. Actively participates in each stage of the process from beginning to completion.
14. Works as a team member with other design professionals.
15. Keeps good records of all business transactions.
16. Writes proposals and all other documentation needed.

Who does a corporate art consultant sell to?
The following are the types of businesses that regularly purchase artwork:
1. Healthcare
2. Hospitality
3. Biotechnology
4. Banking and finance
5. Law
6. Telecommunications

7. Education
8. Commercial Real Estate
9. Professional Sports Teams
10. Defense
11. Government
12. Religious organizations

Other factors to consider

Picture framing business owners sometimes branch out and add art consultation in the hope that it will be a profitable adjunct to their framing business. Does the business owner have the capacity to produce contract framing? Can he/she leave their business during the day to meet with decision makers? Does he/she have sources for artwork? Does he/she have the financial capacity to carry receivables? Does he/she have storage space, delivery vehicles, and installers?

Before expanding into this market, business owners and independent consultants need to understand the big picture. A good banking relationship needs to be in place so that if and when a job with a large budget comes along, the consultant is prepared to close it. Invariably, deposit checks from clients are late; however, deliveries are due and deadlines must be met. Artwork and framing materials must be purchased despite the fact that the client has not sent any money.

Is it feasible to become an art consultant?
1. Can you leave your business?
2. Do you have the capacity to produce, store, and deliver?
3. Do you have a line of credit and a good banking relationship?
4. Do you live in a metropolitan area that can support corporate sales?
5. Do you sell both art and framing?
6. Are you motivated to network and go after the business?
7. Do you have a network of resources such as trained installers, professional printing companies, engravers, and art conservators?

Now that you have a good idea of what an art consultant is and what the profession entails, it is time to discuss the whole process of how it is done. The methods and strategies I write about work for me. I learned these methods by taking risks, learning from mistakes, being professional, keeping a positive attitude, and going after the business. The business a corporate art consultant acquires is constantly shifting with new clients, new artists, new projects, and new challenges. It is a cumulative type of business that builds on experience with some constants and more variables. The following chapters will address both the constants and variables giving insights into how business is done. Enjoy the journey!

Chapter 2

Materials You Will Need to Begin

Be prepared when going into a meeting with a prospective client. Who knows when you may need to measure a wall or photograph the fabric on a chair? Once you have all of the following items, you will be ready to start.

1. Digital camera
2. Tape measure
3. Mat specifier and/or paint fan deck
4. Cell phone with activated voice mail
5. Frame samples
6. Rolling cart
7. Art catalogs and artist binders
8. Printed company information
9. Business cards
10. Notebook, pens, pencils, and Post-it notes
11. Reliable transportation large enough to transport artwork
12. Briefcase
13. Professional wardrobe
14. Computer with email
15. Sleeves to transport artwork
16. Scaled ruler to measure blueprints

After years of carrying catalogs and binders, I finally started using a collapsible rolling cart to carry bulky items. You can purchase one at an office supply store. This cart will help you move most of the items on the materials list and keep you from feeling tired and sweaty before the meeting has begun. I bring my cell phone just in case there is a miscommunication and I need to reach my client. Sometimes a voice message is left on my cell phone notifying me that my client is running late. I turn off my cell phone once I have made contact with the client. It is rude to have your cell phone ringing during a meeting; make a real effort to remember to turn it off.

A digital camera is an incredible tool, and I do not know how I survived before the technology. Not only do I use it at the beginning of a job to have a visual reference of the environment, but I use it to document the different stages of the project. I strongly suggest asking permission before taking photographs. Final installation photographs are taken and downloaded into my computer. Photographs are invaluable and serve several purposes. They are shown to prospective clients when I make presentations. I also use them as support material when I teach classes, write articles, or train consultants. It is a good idea to send photographs to artists for the purpose of showing their framed artwork in the completed project. Photographs of jobs look impressive in company ads and on websites. Art consultants should get in the habit of taking photographs of their projects, from beginning to end.

Basic tools such as a tape measure and mat specifier are used to help gather information at the first meeting. I take wall measurements and write notes that I refer back to when specifying artwork. The mat specifier or paint fan deck is used to match wall colors and fabric samples. Other materials are obvious such as company support material, business cards, writing tools, paper, and a briefcase.

In addition to representing a core group of artists, I recommend obtaining 8 to 10 fine art poster catalogs and becoming familiar with the images each company offers. Many projects will be a combination of fine art and poster art. It is best to bring at least one poster catalog to meetings even if the job calls for all fine art. Invariably, there will be one spot where poster art is needed. It could be a bathroom, employee lounge, or another area where the client wants something on the wall but does not want to spend much money. The following are poster art companies that will provide a full range of imagery for corporate clients. See the References at the back of the book for contact information.

Poster art companies
Editions Limited
Image Conscious
Top Art
Bruce McGaw Graphics
Canadian Art Prints
Bentley Publishing Group
Winn Devon
Poems Art Publishing
New York Graphic Society Publishing Group
Haddad's Fine Arts
Posters International
Wild Apple Graphics
Gango Editions
World Art Group
Rosenstiel's
Third and Wall
Mercurius Art Publishing
Pecheur Images
Bruce Teleky

Acquaint yourself with the latest framing styles and ask for an extra set of corner samples from moulding suppliers to be used in your corporate sales. Often frame samples need to be left with clients on a short-term basis, and you do not want to take samples away from your regular business or a contract framer. Choose the mouldings that are the most suitable for the corporate look and limit them to around 50 corner samples. Get samples of contract mouldings that match current furniture finishes. Generally with contemporary style environments corporate buyers prefer simple, flat, 1" to 3" wood samples that blend with their furniture. In traditional office settings, frame samples will also tend to match the furniture color, but the frames appear more ornate or patterned on the face. Once you have a designated corporate set of frame samples, I suggest removing all of the labels and numbers to guarantee your sources are protected. Create your own labeling system. Offering to show moulding samples with your own labeling system reduces the chances of competitors knowing what frames are specified.

Produce well designed company information to leave with prospects such as a client list, brochure, or a short handout. This reinforces your professional expertise and experience. Naturally, you do not want to overload the prospective client with company information, but you do need to leave material that describes what your capabilities are and a list of which corporate clients you have worked with. An extensive and impressive client list will help set you apart from your competition. When a prospective client reads a client list, quite often there are companies listed that they have done business with. Having mutual clients is a definite advantage in winning them over. It is also a great conversation starter to have the person you are meeting with talk about clients in common. In addition, consider producing a brag book containing photographs of stellar jobs with testimonial letters or even creating a digital photo frame with rotating snapshots.

Investing in a professional wardrobe is an added expense but very necessary. Art consultants project a professional image and need to dress well and be well groomed. This means no jeans even if your client is casual. Many companies have instituted a casual "dress down Friday," but keep a professional appearance regardless of with whom you are meeting. Furthermore, if you are taking an employee with you on a sales appointment, this applies to your employee as well. First impressions are crucial, and you do not want to be dismissed for a poor appearance.

Lastly, a computer with an email account is a necessity. It is a good idea to invest in a computer and printer using an "all-in-one" scanner for color printing, scans, and faxes. All corporate client correspondence and record keeping will be stored in files on your computer. Be sure to back up all of your data regularly. If you are unfamiliar with the basic systems of your computer, take lessons. You will need to use email, know word processing, send attachments, create and maintain files, use PowerPoint, and burn CDs. All of these applications will help you with client communications.

Subscribing to the following industry magazines will also be helpful to keep you informed about what is new in the art, framing, and design industry:

1. Picture Framing Magazine
2. Decor Magazine
3. Art Business News
4. Art World News
5. Healthcare Design Magazine
6. Hospitality Design Magazine

Chapter 3

Networking is a Contact Sport

Those in the art and framing industry who know me understand that I am a strong proponent of networking. Almost everyone networks daily by recommending restaurants, physicians, and stores to their friends. When you discover a "great find," your excitement motivates you to share the experience with others. Similarly, when you encounter a "great find" in a business situation, you tend to spread the word. Networking is spreading the word about your business and exchanging information with successful people. It is putting yourself in situations where successful people surround you. Networking is staying involved and keeping your business name in the spotlight.

In order to successfully network, you will need to put on your sales rep hat and join one or more networking groups. Before discussing networking groups, I want you to grasp the concept of information sharing and talking about your business. To be an effective member of a networking group, you will need to make a convincing argument that persuades others to recommend your business and help you through information sharing.

In order to make a convincing argument about why business people should consider referring your business:

1. You must believe in yourself.
2. You must believe in what you are doing.
3. You must believe in your product and services.
4. You must believe in your company.
5. You must be able to articulate what you do in one or two concise sentences.

What is a networking group?

A networking group is an organization of professional individuals meeting regularly for the purpose of exchanging and sharing information in an effort to grow business. Networking groups are not social clubs. Common goals are to cultivate and establish business friendships, learn about each other's businesses, and enter into a mutually beneficial relationship centered around information sharing. Networking groups usually operate with exclusive member categories posing an attractive incentive for individuals seeking insider business information and timely leads. Meetings may be scheduled weekly, bimonthly, or monthly, before, during, or after business hours. Dues vary according to the type of group but typically range from $300 to $1,500 a year. Members are expected to actively participate and some groups require attendance of at least 50%. Inactive members may be asked to leave making room for a stronger candidate in a particular category. Most networking groups maintain an active website where members can post and review leads. To find out about networking groups, check local business publications and ask professional business people what groups they may recommend.

Joining one or more professional networking groups can potentially offer you many qualified leads and save you hours of research. Who better to exchange leads with than professionals who sell office equipment, plants, interior design services, phone systems, or other services to businesses that are remodeling, expanding, moving, or just opening? Your network associates can supply you with timely contact information and help you grow your business. Networking members will become your allies in the business community, referring companies they know to their clients. Most groups have a directory listing the services of the members. While fellow networking friends are out canvassing the city, they are leaving directories of group members and spreading the word about your business. These networking friends become an invaluable source of information.

When looking for a networking group to join, it is important to visit as a guest to see if the group will be a good fit. Not all networking groups are worthy of your time. Look for a group where you can have the exclusive spot as the art consultant. Observe and gauge the level of professionalism and attendance. Ask members how long they have been in the group, and find out if their sales have increased as a direct result of their membership. Look for a group represented by such professionals as commercial real estate leasing agents, commercial architects, builders, interior designers, and plant and furniture salespeople. Preferably stay away from groups where the majority of members work out of their homes. An effective group should provide you with at least 50 leads a month, not that all of the leads would need your services.

When considering a networking group:
1. Attend the first meeting as a guest.
2. Observe the level of professionalism.
3. Find out the types of businesses represented.
4. Notice how many members attended.
5. Gauge the amount and type of information sharing exchanged.
6. Check for exclusivity in the category of art consultant.
7. Ask members if their business has increased as a direct result of membership.
8. Inquire about the culture of the group.
9. Observe how the members are dressed.

Look for members in these professions:
1. Interior design
2. Architecture
3. Plant sales
4. Furniture sales
5. Commercial real estate
6. Window coverings
7. Flooring and carpet sales
8. Painting
9. Phone systems
10. Security systems
11. Moving companies
12. Computer systems

13. Coffee and vending
14. Landscaping
15. Banking
16. Construction and tenant improvement

Generally avoid groups where the majority of members are in the following categories:
1. Workout trainer
2. Vitamins and nutritional sales
3. Massage therapist
4. Weight loss programs
5. Pet sales
6. Garden supplies
7. Hairstylist
8. Manicure specialist
9. Home based business

Networking skills are simple but must be practiced to achieve your goals. Understand from the outset that networking is a time consuming commitment, and you cannot expect immediate results. Most importantly, show up to meetings and show up prepared with leads to share. It is a give and take arrangement based on information sharing and helping others. Bring contact information to meetings and email members regularly when new contacts arise. If you are in a large networking group, make it a habit to interact with at least three new people each time you attend. When attending a luncheon or dinner, sit next to some-one you have never met before. Make sure to bring business cards and exchange them. It is a good idea to write notes on the back of business cards collected to jog your memory about what was discussed. Be a good listener and get to know as many business professionals as possible. What is important to remember is to take a genuine interest in people before they take an interest in you. Ask people questions about their business. Most art consultants do not utilize networking, so you can use this to your advantage. Networking is a cost effective and powerful personal selling method. If utilized properly, it can grow you business expo-nentially with little cost other than annual dues and your invested time.

Rules of the game of networking
1. Show up regularly and come prepared with leads and information.
2. Bring business cards and make sure your cards identify you as an art consultant.
3. Be a good listener.
4. Meet new people.
5. Take notes.
6. Follow up on leads in a timely manner.
7. Be positive, helpful, and friendly.
8. Project a professional and confident manner.
9. Be willing to take risks.
10. Look for common ground to establish rapport.
11. Do NOT expect immediate results.

12. Communicate well and articulate what you do in a short period of time.
13. Be yourself. Be honest and real.
14. Take a sincere interest in people before you expect them to take an interest in you.
15. Communicate with members regularly, not just at meetings.
16. Form business friendships with members in similar businesses such as architecture, interior design, plant sales, furniture sales, etc.
17. Remember it is not about who you know, but who you are connected to and how those connections will spread the word about your capabilities.
18. Be willing to quit a group if it is not helping you grow your business.
19. Networking is a "contact sport." The more contacts you make, the greater the possibilities for winning more business.

Art consultants should associate with a variety of successful business people. Providing value to other business people will strengthen your network. The more value you provide, the more people will be attracted to you, hence your network expands. Contacts turn into relationships and relationships generate sales. Similarly to adding new artists regularly, you will need to make a steady effort to connect with successful business people. Networking and receiving referrals through contacts with other business professionals will play a crucial role in keeping your business momentum going.

This type of doing business is based on business friendships that are maintained and nurtured in a way very similar to personal friendships. Business friends help each other out by providing information, leads, referrals, sources, and problem solving. By positioning yourself as a networking individual constantly meeting new people in the business community, you are building a network of influential individuals. They will not only use your business, but will also refer business to you. Networking involves developing a mindset that successful sales people use to gain access to the movers and shakers in their local business communities. How can art consultants raise their visibility and bid on more jobs? Simply by becoming an active networker, the likelihood of finding out about opportunities is far greater than if you were not networking at all.

At networking meetings and events, you have face-to-face contact with influential and motivated people. At one American Society of Interior Designers (ASID) event in San Diego, there was a networking event called Speed Dating Networking. Each interior designer had 3 minutes to talk with an Industry Partner (professionals that support and join ASID), and then a buzzer went off and each participant was teamed up with the next person, and so on for approximately one and a half hours. In that period of time, business cards and information were exchanged with a core group of professionals (an equal number of designers to industry partners) needing art consultation and other design services. The beauty of this type of event was that people came together for the purpose of networking and making connections. A prequalified group of individuals spent time openly communicating to learn about each other. There was no other agenda but to network. Think of how much time it would take on the phone to have an equal amount of interaction.

What qualities make a business person a good networker?
1. Friendly

2. Helpful
3. Patient (keep expectations realistic)
4. Resourceful, well connected, and informed
5. Good listener
6. Good memory
7. Organized
8. Projects professional image
9. Motivated
10. Genuine
11. Inquisitive
12. Appreciative
13. Tenacious
14. Manages time effectively
15. Risk taker
16. Participatory
17. Supportive of others
18. Giver, willing to share information
19. Not afraid to ask for information
20. Someone who gives feedback, credit, and gives thanks when due

My experience with networking groups

I admit to being skeptical of business networking groups in the past. However, this all changed in 2002 when I became a member of a San Diego based networking group called Entransa. The members were sales representatives motivated and willing to share information about their accounts and what businesses were signing leases and spending money on tenant improvements. Information discussed centered around companies to call on and who the decision makers were on large projects. As information was exchanged and members assisted each other, business friendships were established.

From these business relationships, two things happened that had a tremendous benefit to my business. I was receiving referrals from two levels—from networking friends from the group and from decision makers that were extremely happy with the quality of my work. It then became apparent to me that networking and referrals were hugely significant to growing my business. Ideally, I could grow my business exponentially by making more business friends. Physically getting out of my business to network meant the difference between staying in business and going out of business.

The momentum I received as a result of leads and referrals from networking contacts made my business stronger and more solid. I became sold on the benefits of networking, and the fact that my competitors were not making appearances at the types of events I frequented motivated me even more to push harder. My next step was to join other networking groups. At one time I was involved in 3, but upon evaluation 2 groups seemed a better balance for me. It is important to try new groups in your community and find the best groups where you can secure the exclusive spot in the category of art consultant. It is through my networking groups that I made excellent connections leading to jobs that I would otherwise not have known about.

Art consultants should also join their local chapter of ASID, which is not a networking group but an organization to support with potential for making contacts. If your competitors are members of ASID, you should definitely join as well.

The concept of networking sounds simple: make business friends and be helpful. It is simple, but the key is to make a conscious effort to be a giver and stay involved. I show up at networking events open to all kinds of businesses, and while I meet furniture reps, lawyers, architects, graphic designers, and plant vendors, I do not see art consultants or gallery owners. I have a captive audience of people to network with and spread the word about what I do. My strategy is to keep my expectations realistic and emotions in check. I routinely try to be on the giving side, especially at the beginning of a business relationship. I focus and listen to others talk about their business without interrupting. Naturally, the best way to move the relationship along is to show interest and share information. By being on the giving side, the human response usually is to give back and spread the word about your business. People want to feel good about giving, and when a business friendship has been formed you will be astonished with the amount of referrals and leads that will come your way.

There are many ways to be helpful to your business friends, which include giving leads, sending newspaper clippings about their companies or colleagues, discussing common business concerns, and sending business their way. By presenting yourself as a helpful person interested in advancing other people's sales, you will receive a constant flow of referrals in return. Bob Burg says it best in his book, *Endless Referrals*. Burg states, "All things being equal, people will do business with, and refer business to, those people they know, like, and trust."

Each business friend you make comes with a network of contacts, potentially providing extreme value to you. As you grow, these business relationships based on trust, mutual admiration, and respect provide you access to new networks. Most professionals have at least 200 people in their network. Obviously not all of these contacts will need an art consultant, but by adding new business friends constantly, you are leveraging yourself into being on the receiving end of referrals. Think of it this way. If a decision maker needs an art consultant and they know someone who knows you but not your competitor, who has the advantage? You do. Your influence is being spread through many business networks.

This is a true story where a networking friend referred me for a job. We had plans to meet at a wine tasting event that was part of our networking organization. Since my friend had recently moved, she was spending the night at a small boutique hotel. When I heard where she was staying, I said, "That place has a wonderful location but sure could use some remodeling. Why don't you find out when they expect to renovate the rooms?" The next morning my friend called at 8:30 a.m. and told me she had found out from the manager that the hotel was planning a major renovation. My friend gave the manager my information and called to give me the contact's phone number. The manager was new to San Diego and did not know any art consultants. I was able to close the job without my competitors even knowing a job existed. Insider information is enormously beneficial, and I can speak from experience that these kinds of interactions happen frequently through networking contacts and give you an edge over your competition.

Successful networking takes a blend of people skills, intuition, and business savvy. Professionals look for enthusiastic people with whom they can maintain relationships and count on for high quality services and good value. They prefer establishing a relationship with a business owner and hearing stories about how the business has progressed over the years. Networking meetings provide a relaxed environment where guards are lowered and business people can get to know each other in a more relaxed setting.

Bringing your best clients to networking events is another strategy to consider. My networking groups host golf tournaments, wine tasting events, and a day at the races. I bring my best clients as my guest to one or more of these events. This helps solidify the relationship and is a way of showing appreciation for the business relationship. Getting to know your client outside of a work environment at a networking event is a great way to mix fun with business. It shows you are not solely interested in the business aspect of the relationship, but you want to get to know them as a person.

It is never too late to join a networking group and begin attending business functions. I was in business for more than 20 years before I discovered the benefits of networking and referrals. Reading books on the subjects of networking, referrals, and how to sell will energize you and help you do it the right way. There are free business e-zines full of tips and ideas. I find reading weekly e-zines reaffirms my methods, and I suggest you take advantage of these free sources. My final word about networking is that the best thing that has come out of my networking group (Entransa) is that in our monthly discussions, if someone wants to know a contact at a specific business, he/she asks and at least one person responds with the information needed. This information is golden. Do your due diligence and find the best possible networking group in your area. It will make a huge difference in your success as a corporate art consultant. Until you witness the process, it is difficult to fully grasp its value. Networking provides momentum for business growth allowing you to surpass competitors stalled in the marketplace.

Networking groups to consider joining
IFMA (International Facility Management Association) ifma.org
BOMA (Building Owners and Managers Association) boma.org
BNI (Business Networking International) bni.com
Chamber of Commerce
CREW (Commercial Real Estate Women) crewnetwork.org
Rotary
Le Tip
LinkedIn Groups specific to your city

What is it going to cost?
Costs will vary depending on which group you join and how often the group meets. The following are costs to consider when joining one or more networking groups:

1. Dues
2. Events
3. Wardrobe and grooming
4. Transportation
5. Professional material

6. Meals
7. Donations and sponsorships

To summarize, what is networking?

1. Sharing information about your company with other professionals.
2. Helping other business people grow their business.
3. Putting yourself in situations surrounded by successful and motivated individuals.
4. Staying involved and keeping your name in the spotlight.
5. Making connections with the right people.
6. Interacting with successful business professionals regularly in meetings and at events.
7. Physically getting out of your business and going after new business by constantly making and adding business friends.

Chapter 4

Social Networking

In today's age of immediate information technology, art consultants who have a presence on LinkedIn, Twitter, Facebook, Plaxo, or other social networking sites are one step ahead of their competition. By joining one or more of these sites, art consultants can have a free online presence, communicate with contacts regularly, find new artists, promote their business, list their website, and receive recommendations. The use of social networking sites by business owners is huge and growing exponentially every day.

LinkedIn is set up to organize contacts and promote your business. The first step is to complete a profile listing details about your position, company, education, work experience, and interests. Upload a photograph and invite business contacts to connect with you. LinkedIn is a great marketing tool and a way to discover new contacts that may need art consultation services. The site allows you to develop a network of contacts referred to as connections. Added by mutual consent, users of LinkedIn may not only view their own connections (second degree of separation) but they can view the connections of their connections (third degree of separation) putting them in touch with another layer of potential high level people to interact with. This third degree of separation opens opportunities to explore new contacts and expose your professional information. Upon request, the user can ask for their mutual contact to introduce them, thus easing the barrier to communication.

When I collect business cards from networking events, the following day I request to connect with these business people on LinkedIn. Through the site, it is easy to send emails to your connections, some of whom otherwise have hard emails to remember. Invariably, people tend to move from company to company and change emails, but people do update their LinkedIn information making it easy to follow them. Another feature of LinkedIn is the ability for members to join groups with like-minded individuals. In these groups, you can find artists, interior designers, architects, and other professionals that should know about you. Group members post questions and comments about business related subjects opening up a forum to exchange ideas and information. For example, LinkedIn has groups called Creative Art Consultants, Healthcare Fine Art, Professional Fine Art Network, and Fine Art in the Workplace. By joining these LinkedIn groups, you have access to numerous professionals who are involved in the arts. If you are looking for new artists, these groups may be a goldmine.

In San Diego, I attend a LinkedIn based networking group with other business people. The members meet at different venues around the city to network. Since LinkedIn has brought us together, we exchange tips and strategies about using LinkedIn. Recently, I came away from a meeting with several excellent contacts and three leads of companies needing artwork. The use of LinkedIn has saved me time and effort in discovering who is spending money in San Diego. Speaking with others about the current economy and exchanging business stories sets the stage for making more networking business friends.

The San Diego Business LinkedIn events are advantageous because the members embody extensive backgrounds from business owners and executives to scientists and writers. Whereas my other networking organizations operate with members representing certain categories, LinkedIn meetings have a much broader range of businesses because there are no membership fees or exclusivity restrictions. Different people attend each function. The point is to keep your networking options open and mix it up. The key is to actively go after the business instead of expecting it to come to you. Finding and attending groups through LinkedIn can be an excellent way to gain practice and learn networking skills.

Art consultants using social networking position themselves higher in Google and Yahoo searches. Another popular social site is Twitter, which allows the user to send a short message of 140 characters to a group of approved followers. Again, this is an excellent way to disseminate information about what is new and exciting in your business. On Twitter you identify yourself by setting up a personal user name and then using that name you send out a "tweet," which is a short message. You can follow others on Twitter keeping an ongoing dialogue with people in as many areas of interest as you like. The time commitment is whatever you want it to be. I have the name "Artnetworker" on Twitter and my messages may mention tips for artists on networking to exciting projects I am completing. Also by using specific words in "tweets" you may increase your search engine optimization. Every bit of exposure helps.

Facebook is less businesslike than LinkedIn but still another social media site worth investigating, especially when trying to connect with younger clients. Many artists post their portfolios on Facebook. Business owners can have their own Fan Page, connecting with clients, friends, and family who become their "fans." Products can be featured and pictures posted. Ads can be purchased on Facebook and linked to websites to attract new potential clients. It is important to understand that the use of Facebook by the younger generation is a way of life entrenched in their way of communicating. Instead of using the telephone, the youth of today send text messages and update their Facebook page. As these individuals enter the business world, their habits of communication will impact how business is done.

Social networking is an excellent way for art consultants to reach out and broaden their business network. By connecting with others on social media sites, you are increasing your visibility and branding your company. It is also an excellent way to remind existing clients of your services. In addition, you can connect with clients outside of your geographic area. Unlike the cost of maintaining and upgrading a business website, social networking will help you grow your business at no cost other than your own time commitment. Social networking is a phenomenon that is on the rise as a way of marketing and interacting with business professionals. It is no longer just for the generation of texting and instant messaging youth. Social networking has grown into an essential component of routine business, and it should not be overlooked as a vital tool that once explored and implemented will definitely raise visibility.

Clearly, the younger generation buys through websites and communicates through social networking sites. If you recall not too long ago business owners had to adapt to using fax machines and acclimate to using email. As the youth of today enter the work force, their buying patterns and communication will transition into using social media sites to gather information in their decision making process. Business owners too are transitioning from print ads to digital media. Never has it been so easy to promote yourself and your products by engaging in the digital world. Social media sites offer a virtual sea of knowledge and endless possibilities to engage with clients on so many levels. The best part is that it is free and easy to navigate. Take the time to become a part of social networking. We are fortunate these avenues exit in today's business world. When I started working in the 1980s, the ability to reach out and convey a specific message worldwide was beyond comprehension. Seriously consider taking part in the technology to reach out and communicate with others, especially when it is easy and free. Though it is difficult to actually measure the results of social networking, art consultants should start using one or more sites in an effort to increase business and visibility.

The following are advantages of using social networking sites:
1. Increase your visibility and let people know who you are and what you do.
2. Promote your products and services at no cost other than your own time.
3. Broaden your client base and business network.
4. Position yourself in Google and Yahoo searches.
5. Learn from experts and exchange information.
6. Join business networking groups with no annual membership.
7. Connect with younger clients who use social networking daily.
8. Reach clients outside of your geographic area.
9. Provide exposure to reconnect with existing client base.
10. Interact with like-minded individuals.
11. Join groups with specific interests to find new artists and additional sources.
12. Organize your contacts and keep track of people as they move and change email addresses.
13. Helps to establish you as an expert.

Chapter 5

Finding Leads and Getting Referrals

As a corporate art consultant, you need to be a well informed, connected member of your local business community, which is essential in your constant search for new business. Leads generate sales, which is basically a numbers game. The more leads you call on, the better chance you have for setting up appointments. The more appointments scheduled, the better chance you have to close sales.

Leads come from a variety of sources. It is important to actively seek out leads by joining at least one professional networking group and reading local publications to see what businesses have recently leased office space. Then you must follow up on those leads by getting on the phone. Talk to interior designers, project managers, architects, business owners, and facility managers about projects in the pipeline. When reading local publications, look for the names of clients you may have crossed paths with before. By reading an article about one of my residential clients in a local business journal, I was able to set up an appointment because the business owner knew my business and me. The relationship led to multiple jobs and ongoing purchases with a growing company. Had I not taken the initiative to make contact, chances are I would not have been on board with the company and one of my competitors would be servicing the account.

There are a myriad of ways to find leads. A combination of methods works best, including belonging to networking groups, sharing information with other business professionals, reading business publications, looking at signage for new buildings, engaging in social networking, conducting ongoing marketing, scheduling lunch and learns, getting involved in community service, and contacting your friends and neighbors. Think of it like a funnel that needs to be constantly filled at the top. By making a conscious effort to seek new contacts daily and following up on leads, you will achieve success. If you do not keep adding contacts and calling on leads to expand your client base, the pipeline will run dry.

Leads versus referrals

There is a difference between referrals and leads. When someone gives you a referral, the contact person is expecting your call. Referral appointments are usually easier to close. Seize the opportunity to call for an appointment immediately. When you follow up on a referral, you are putting someone else's reputation at risk. Hence, if you do not act like a professional and follow up in a timely manner, this poor conduct will get back to the person who referred you. Not only will you make that person look bad, but most likely you will be cut off from future referrals. The important fact to remember is that a person of influence has prequalified you as a worthy source. With a referral, chances are you may be the only person meeting with the decision maker, therefore closing the job should be easier than with other appointments.

A person of influence in the business community who has high regard for you has helped remove some obstacles, clearing the path to success. A positive performance on your part will have a snowball effect, as referrals will keep coming your way. Always keep the person who gave you the referral in the loop and communicate with him or her about the progress of the project. More importantly, thank the person for the referral. Business people like helping others succeed, but they want their efforts to be recognized. A written thank you note goes a long way in showing gratitude to someone who has referred business to you. Handwritten notes are rare these days, and taking the extra effort to send one will register quite positively with the recipient.

When someone gives you a lead, it is information and should be treated as a cold call. During my seminars, I am often asked about a conflict of interest in sharing client information with networking members. From my point of view, there is no conflict of interest. Group members share leads and make a point when calling to NOT say where the lead came from. This is common networking etiquette. Rarely has anyone I have cold called asked me where I received the information that they were moving, expanding, or remodeling. If asked, I simply say the information "came across my desk." Keep in mind that project managers expect calls from sales representatives; it comes with the territory. Discussions at networking meetings center around what project managers are doing and how to contact them.

Lunch and Learns

If you strategize well and connect with decision makers, business will come your way. One excellent method to get in front of decision makers is to schedule a "Lunch and Learn" at the key design firms in your area. Although it will take time to meet with all of them, if you schedule one or two a month over a period of a few years, you will cover the majority of them. New design firms open every year, and it is up to you to know who the designers are and what they do. Design firms are architectural firms that usually have an interior design department.

In addition, contact interior design firms that work on corporate projects. Schedule an hour meeting, buy the staff lunch, pitch your services, show artwork, and ask for their business. Prepare a PowerPoint presentation showing your stellar jobs, and discuss your capabilities. Design firms are working on corporate projects and should definitely know about you as a source. This is a very cost effective way to have face-to-face contact with design professionals as well as an excellent way to get leads and referrals. In many cases, design firms are using one of your competitors as an art consultant, and if you do not take the initiative to meet with them to consider you as a source, chances are your competitor will keep getting their business. Keep in mind, the more sources a design firm has the better. Perhaps their current art consultant cannot help them with a certain situation and you can.

The point is to move forward and meet with as many design professionals as possible. Generally these meetings have anywhere from 3 to 15 design professionals attending. The set up is usually in a conference room where there is room to show artwork and do a PowerPoint presentation. Bring a good representation of artwork and support material. Exchange business cards and stay in contact with the people you meet. Lunch and Learns are invaluable and getting an appointment to set one up is fairly easy. Remember, it is all about getting the word out about your services and meeting prospective clients.

Building signage

Another way to get leads is to look at signage of new corporate buildings being built. If a new corporate center or medical facility is under construction, look at the signage and write down contact information. Signage often lists contractors and phone numbers. Call and ask who the project manager is or who is responsible for the artwork for the facility. Also, when you are working in a building, look around and see if any tenant improvement projects are under way.

Canvas the building and look for signs on suites indicating who is moving in. If you are working on a project in a building, ask your contact person if he/she knows any information about new occupants. Do not be afraid to ask questions. This is another way to find leads, and if you are already at a building anyway, taking an extra few minutes to investigate may be very useful in the information obtained. You can also take a snapshot with a digital camera so you do not have to write everything down. Bring this information to your networking meetings. Remember that just because a lead may not be useful to you does not mean it will not be valuable to someone else in your networking group.

In-house signage and marketing

If your company has a showroom with retail foot traffic, putting up a sign that states you offer art consultation can help generate leads. Some of your retail clients may not realize your company offers corporate art consultation. Display a sign in prominent areas of your showroom. This can be done with simply putting a sign in a photo frame on the design counter or more elaborately by framing a sign to hang on the wall. Your print ads should also market your art consultation services. Our company has received several great contacts as a direct result of ads placed in the design resource guide of a local magazine and in the San Diego chapter of the American Society of Interior Designers (ASID) newsletter. The local ASID newsletter is a valuable and informative quarterly publication in which to place cost effective ads to target an audience needing art consultation services. Also consider a direct marketing campaign to architects, interior designers, and project managers with follow up appointment setting phone calls.

Pay-for-lead services

Another way to find leads is to pay a monthly fee to a company that supplies lead information. These companies can be found on the Internet, and if you want a constant supply of information about businesses moving, you may want to investigate these services. I found out about these types of services through one of my networking groups. Moving companies and real estate leasing agents often will subscribe to acquire monthly listings to assist with their businesses. Pay-for-lead companies supply information to specific geographic areas including when leases are up and moving dates. Phone numbers and contacts are listed with each entry. Prices for this information may be steep, but you will get a constant stream of useful data.

Artists

Ask your artists what projects they are working on. Where else are they selling their artwork? If your artists are connected to other design professionals, it is good information to have. Attend functions your artists invite you to and network effectively. Find out what people of influence your artists know, and make an effort to meet new connections. Again, the more people who know about you, the better chance you have of spreading the word about your services.

Friends, neighbors, and vendors

Your neighbors and friends are sources of leads as well. Do not be timid about asking whether or not they may know of any companies that need your services. Find out where your friends work, and should they indeed be able to put you in contact with decision makers on a project, ask for an introduction. Make sure your circle of friends knows what you do and what type of clients you service. Also be in contact with your insurance provider, attorney, accountant, and other professionals whom you pay for services. Why should your accountant or attorney be using another art consultant? Keep the communication open when meeting with your attorney, banker, accountant, or any other professional and ask if they may need art consultation. These professionals should be using your services and referring business to you. Again, unless you ask for introductions and ask for the business, the chances are new business that is within your sphere of influence may not come your way.

Networking groups

Networking groups will provide you with a constant stream of leads. Join at least one networking group and attend meetings regularly. A previous chapter of this book is devoted to the relationship between art consultation and networking in terms of business growth. The importance of finding an effective networking group and using it to your advantage cannot be understated. It is critical to achieving success.

Social networking

The concept of using social networking to increase contacts was also explored in a previous chapter of this book. Sites such as LinkedIn provide free exposure for business people, and art consultants should participate. It may be difficult to actually measure the benefits of social networking sites, but considering it is free, the chances are if used judiciously, the benefits will outweigh the invested time for setup and ongoing participation.

Telemarketing

Calling on the phone is time consuming but definitely pays off. One cold call I made to a biotechnology firm resulted in a $30,000 sale. The administrator I spoke with was too busy to find an art consultant, and when I called the timing was perfect. She was new to the area and did not know how to go about finding a professional to assist her with selecting artwork for their facility. My competitors did not even know about this job, because my contact took immediate action to meet with me and turn over the project with confidence that it would be done right. I have kept in touch with this administrator since she has moved to another company. Staying in touch with your contact is crucial. Contacts do not always tell you if they are moving, but by asking questions you can usually find them, especially if you have a good business relationship.

Set aside at least two hours of uninterrupted time per week to call prospective clients. Sometimes you will feel like an investigator, asking a lot of questions, trying to find out pertinent information, and leaving numerous voice messages. Calling on the phone makes a big difference in finding decision makers who are looking for an art consultant. Project enthusiasm in your voice. If your community has a business journal, it most likely prints an annual publication, or Book of Lists, listing the top companies by professional field, with phone numbers. Call people listed such as bankers, builders, architects, interior designers, and medical institutions. Call the facilities managers of the fastest growing companies listed in the Book of Lists. Ask if they are expanding, remodeling, or moving in the near future.

In this process, you will leave many voice mails and reach only a portion of the decision makers, but remember you are planting the seed in the minds of those you do reach. Again, it is a numbers game and the more calls you make the more chances you have to reach interested parties. Some companies will be interested in your services, but it may be too early in the project to consider artwork. Find out when would be the best time to call back and follow through with a second call. Keep the information in your tickler file and follow up. You can invest in a computer software program or use index cards to organize the leads and information in your tickler file. The most common reason that many leads do not turn into appointments is the lack of repeated follow up phone calls.

The leads you receive from networking meetings are essentially wasted unless you make an effort to get on the phone. The insider information obtained at these meetings is time sensitive. Focus on the most promising prospects needing your services. I can vouch for the return on investment from my networking groups, because I spend time each week calling the leads I receive. By telemarketing, I constantly set up appointments with companies I know need artwork. Being informed about where money is being spent and who to contact keeps me focused on where to concentrate my efforts. In order to succeed as an art consultant, telemarketing must be a routine practice. Consider the alternative. If your competitors are telemarketing and regularly landing new accounts as a result, who has the advantage/disadvantage?

You will be surprised at who returns your calls. I have made many excellent contacts by cold calling, and some of the best jobs I have ever worked on came from cold calling. I keep my expectations realistic, and when I get returned calls I am intrigued by the element of surprise. After most telemarketing sessions, I have at least one interested person who calls me back. I can never predict who will call me back, but I can vouch that my efforts do pay off. This method has worked well for me over the years, and I do not have a problem with getting on the phone. Rarely has anyone been rude or treated me unfairly. What I have found is that project managers expect to be called. It comes with the territory. I have found several project managers simply by being on the phone, asking questions, and leaving voice mail messages.

Another point to ponder is that just because a project manager has a relationship with an existing art consultant does not mean that they will not consider meeting with you and using your services on future projects. More than once I have been called to work on a project because the previous art consultant messed up. Being number two can have an advantage. I have also been called when a design committee wanted something fresh and felt their previous art consultant was showing the same thing over and over. It is not always about selling new art or framing. Large facilities, especially hospitals, need art consultants to maintain the existing artwork. Periodic calls from facilities managers will require art consultants to fix pieces with broken glass, scratched acrylic, or damaged frames. Being service oriented will help you win over accounts.

Remaining positive and unemotional when telemarketing may be difficult at first. I distance myself from the telemarketing process, and I do not have any expectations. It is a numbers game and each call is one step toward getting an appointment. From experience, I know telemarketing works in conjunction with other methods of spreading the word about services I offer. Keeping in contact with clients by checking in with them on the phone periodically shows them you are interested in maintaining the relationship. It also gives you information about contacts moving to another company and consequently who has taken their place. Telemarketing takes concentration and discipline. Again, if your competitors are following up on leads by telemarketing and you are not, why give them an advantage? Part of your success is defined by your willingness to telemarket, network, or do whatever it takes to go after new business.

Tips for telemarketing:
1. Devote a minimum of 2 hours a week to be on the phone.
2. Turn off your cell phone.
3. Disable call waiting.
4. Be organized and take good notes. Keep records of whom you spoke with, the date, and what was discussed. If you left a message, document it for future reference.
5. Start with calling companies that you know are moving, expanding, or remodeling. These will be leads from your networking group.
6. If you get a voice mail, leave a brief message stating the reason you called and include your phone number.
7. Do not call on the phone when you are tired or not feeling well.
8. Do not call first thing Monday or after 1:00 pm on Friday. It is best not to call during lunch hours.
9. Use a friendly, upbeat tone. Speak clearly.
10. Try to get to the decision maker. Networking friends can usually give you this information. Treat it as a cold call unless it is a referral.
11. Do not expect immediate results.
12. If you are the business owner, let them know. Decision makers prefer working with business owners.
13. Follow up on leads where interest was expressed but it was too early to consider artwork.

What to say on the phone
Telemarketing can be frustrating, tricky, time consuming, and challenging all at one time. The best approach is to remain positive, stay detached emotionally yet with realistic expectations, and be committed to keep doing it. Knowing what to say and how to get past the

gatekeeper will help improve your success rate. The goal is to find the decision maker and set up an appointment. Using some of these techniques will make telemarketing not seem so dreadful.

Getting past the gatekeeper:

1. Ask for the facilities department. If you know of a specific project, ask who the decision maker is and get their name.
2. Ask for the correct spelling of the person's name. If you cannot tell the gender by the name, ask politely.
3. Once you have the name of the decision maker, ask to speak directly to that person.
4. Briefly introduce yourself, mention the project, and ask if you can set up a meeting to discuss the art requirements for the project.
5. Leave a voice message if the person is unavailable. Speak clearly and leave your name and phone number. Repeat your phone number again at the end of the message.
6. Concentrate on calling people networking members have informed you are currently working on projects.
7. Do not be afraid to ask questions, especially when speaking to a receptionist or operator.
8. If you are trying to speak to a particular person and the gatekeeper asks you to state the reason for your call, say it is regarding a bid, purchase, or particular project.
9. Should you get lost in phone menus requesting extensions, try pressing O for the operator. If you have a name but not an extension, ask the operator for the extension or direct number.
10. When you make contact with an interested person, be respectful of their time. Remember your objective is to get an appointment. Be focused and polite. Do not go on and on about your capabilities. Set the appointment, say thanks, and end the dialogue.
11. Try asking, "Who is responsible for the interior environment of your office?"
12. Try asking, "Who in your company will be coordinating the art program for your new space?"
13. Try asking, "Who is responsible for the art and framing purchases at your company?"
14. Try asking, "Do you use framed artwork in your facility? If so, would you please direct me to that person?"

Timing

Leads can be cold or warm. Warm leads means the business has a definite need at the moment you receive the information. This is not the case with cold leads. If you have a warm or even hot lead, call the contact person immediately. The longer you wait to call, the less apt you are to schedule an appointment because warm leads turn cold quickly. Do not give your competition an opportunity to get in before you. Timing and a bit of luck do come into play when an art consultant is trying to find out who needs artwork for a particular project. Keep a tickler file and refer back to it on a regular basis making calls according to your notes. Remember, most opportunities do not lead to sales because of a lack of follow through. This coupled with a disregard for timing tends to leave many untapped sales opportunities open. Stay on top of your leads, especially the ones with the best prospects for closure.

Sources for leads and contacts:

1. Networking groups
2. Business publications
3. Personal friends, neighbors, and artists
4. Signage on buildings under construction
5. Information sharing with business friends
6. Lunch and Learn meetings at design firms
7. Book of Lists
8. Telemarketing
9. Social networking
10. Signage at your business
11. Advertising your services
12. Pay for leads services

Chapter 6

Appointments, Meetings, and Presentations

The most common way to set an appointment is by phone, though quite often appointments are made through email. When scheduling an appointment, I ask my contact person what is convenient for them, and I have them suggest the date and time. If I know certain days will not work I will say, "I am busy on Wednesday and Friday morning but the rest of the week I am free. What works for you?" I do not schedule more than two appointments per business day. Preparation and being on time is imperative. Always confirm your appointment at least one day prior to the meeting. Since corporate business people are quite busy, I schedule the appointment at their work place. I remain very flexible should appointments need to be rescheduled or my contact is running late.

While you have the contact on the phone setting the appointment, ask some key questions to get an idea of the scope of the project. You do not want to ask too many questions, but in turn you need to qualify that you will be meeting with the decision maker(s) and to assure them that you can take care of the project.

There are two kinds of appointments: selling appointments and company introduction appointments. In a company introduction appointment, such as a Lunch and Learn, your objective is to educate other design professionals about your capabilities so they will consider you for future projects. Since you are not there to discuss a specific project, you will focus on the services you offer, artists you represent, and past experience. Have a PowerPoint presentation of no longer than 30 minutes to show specific jobs in a variety of different settings. Company introduction meetings play a key role in obtaining new clients. Schedule these during slow periods, but do schedule them. Leave promotional material, get business cards, and follow up by contacting these individuals quarterly.

Selling appointments require more concentration. Since there is more at stake than with company introduction meetings, you will need to mentally prepare yourself for getting into the selling mode. The first meeting with a prospective client is where first impressions are formed. It is your opportunity to sell yourself and your company. Capitalize on this opportunity by asking the right questions, taking thorough notes, and getting a feel for the scope of the job. When you are meeting at the actual office space that needs artwork, ask for a tour of the facility. Discuss art placement and the kinds of artwork that may work in the space to get feedback from your prospect. Ask for a floor plan or blueprints. If none are available, make sketches, measure walls, and do not be afraid to ask for extra time to get all of the information you need. Match the wall colors to your mat specifier so you can coordinate framing design. Write down fabric colors and furniture finishes. The more details you note, the easier it will be to design the job. Take digital photographs once you have been granted permission to do so. Unfortunately with corporate art consultation you will be spending time bidding on projects with no guarantee of closing the job. The more experience you have diagnosing and recommending solutions the higher your ratio of closing jobs will be.

Each job presents a different set of circumstances. In most cases, I do not bring an extensive amount of artwork and catalogs to the first meeting. However, on smaller jobs I will bring what I need to close the sale. Bring company support material including a current client list and either a brochure or fact sheet about your company. I start the meeting by giving out my client list and support material. Quite often the person I am meeting with will look over the client list and talk to me about clients we have in common. This is a great way to break the ice and establish rapport.

Following a brief discussion about who I am and what I do, I proceed to discuss the project. With repeat clients, I start the meeting with an informal exchange of pleasantries before delving into business. I try to create a relaxed dialogue. Usually, choosing artwork is fun and a diversion from the prospect's usual work routine. After obtaining the necessary information and discussing possible visions for the project, it is time to wrap up the meeting. Usually with small projects, art selections can be made without the need for a second meeting. Remain sensitive to the prospect's time limitations, and do not prolong the meeting. Before leaving, be sure to exchange business cards and make an effort to set up a second meeting should one be necessary.

Some jobs will require only one or two meetings to get to the proposal stage while other jobs will require many meetings to reach the proposal stage. Regardless, at the second meeting you will actually present a large selection of artwork, show frame samples, and review artist binders. After much consideration about which artists to show for the space, the next step is to pull a selection of artwork and transport it to the second meeting. If at all possible, bring an employee with you to assist in moving and showing the artwork. Working with another team member is much easier. I put the artwork in protective plastic sleeves that hold artwork up to 40 x 50 paper size. Larger artwork I roll in brown paper. At all times I make sure the artwork is protected.

The second meeting is a getting down to business meeting. Many decisions will be made including the quantity of pieces, art selection, framing design, art placement, budget, turnaround time, installation, and any art commissions for the project. Remember the prospect is relying on your expertise to make suggestions and assure the project runs smoothly. After showing artwork and artist binders, make a stack of artwork that the decision maker is interested in and separate the rejected artwork. Use Post-it notes to tag images from the artist binders and poster catalogs. Mark the floor plan or blueprint with the pieces selected before preparing to leave. Should another meeting be necessary, inquire about scheduling it before leaving.

Meetings generally run approximately one hour long unless it is a large project. I always arrive at appointments early knowing it takes time to unload sleeves of artwork. Be sure to turn off your cell phone. Always be very polite to the receptionist and get his/her name. Ask the receptionist if you can set up in a conference room where you can spread out your materials. When you return for the second meeting, call the receptionist by name and act friendly. Also, when calling the company, it makes a better impression to greet the receptionist by name.

If a meeting is to begin at 10:00 a.m., I will be sitting in the reception area waiting at

9:55 a.m. with all of my materials with me. When I am at the art selection phase of a project, I arrive early and ask to set up in the meeting room with all of the artwork ready to show. I do not want to appear tense or tired from unloading and setting up, so I allow ample time. Should my prospective client offer to help me unload, I never accept. I jokingly say that moving the artwork around keeps me in shape.

Some presentations will be scheduled with a committee of decision makers to interview you for a new project. The case may be that several art consultants are being interviewed with the purpose of narrowing down whom the committee would like to work with. In this situation, it may be advantageous to have a PowerPoint presentation with actual photographs depicting your stellar jobs. Bring a selection of suitable artwork and company support material. Communicate with excitement, be dynamic, and address creative solutions with confidence.

The more appointments and meetings you attend, the more confident and relaxed you will become. When I first started making appointments, I was always younger than the decision makers. Unfortunately age can be a factor in choosing a consultant. Younger professionals are sometimes dismissed for lack of experience. Try not to get discouraged, and realize each job is a stepping stone to a larger job. Even if you are not rewarded the contract, you have gained valuable experience.

Points to consider about meetings:

1. Most corporate clients never visit your location.
2. Confirm meetings at least 24 hours prior to the scheduled time.
3. Be conscious of your client/prospect time limitations.
4. Be flexible about scheduling and work around the other person's schedule.
5. Take accurate notes while you are at the meeting.
6. Bring more artwork and frame samples than will work because you cannot predict responses.
7. Arrive early and bring an assistant when possible.
8. Avoid accepting help in loading and unloading artwork from your prospective client.
9. Protect the artwork at all times.
10. Schedule both selling meetings and company introduction meetings.
11. Learn the reception's name and use it. Make an effort to be friendly to the receptionist.
12. Have a PowerPoint presentation ready showing stellar jobs.

Chapter 7

Proposals and Quotations

Once the art and framing selections have been chosen, the next step is to prepare a written proposal detailing the job specifications. This should include an art description, art location, size of artwork, framing specifications, price per piece, installation requirements, terms of payment, and turnaround time. Smaller and less complicated jobs have fairly straightforward and simple proposals. Larger jobs, such as hospital art programs, require visuals of the pieces being proposed, written text about the purpose of the art program, line-by-line itemization of expenses and reimbursables, and other pertinent information to the job.

Some companies will send out a RFP (request for proposal) to 3 or more art consultants for a job. The RFP will outline the scope of the work needed. Preparing a proposal is a very time-consuming process with no guarantee of being awarded a contract. Blueprints and/or elevations are distributed, and the art consultant is given a deadline to submit his/her vision for the master art program. Sometimes art consultants will walk through the construction site to get a better understanding of the building layout. Consultants are given access to fabric samples and color boards detailing specific areas of the facility. Preparation for a RFP usually takes 2 to 4 weeks or more depending on the time line and scale of the project. A committee makes decisions once each consultant has made an art presentation and completed the RFP requirements.

Quotations are used for pricing purposes on smaller jobs where a purchase order needs to be generated rather than a contract being signed. These are sent electronically or faxed to the client. Once a purchase order arrives, the job can begin. If the corporation does not use purchase orders, a signed and approved proposal will give you the green light to proceed. It is prudent to have everything in writing and not to proceed merely on a verbal approval.

Pricing jobs can be tricky, and there are many factors to consider such as the quantity of pieces, type of artwork, production aspect to the framing, and dimension of the pieces specified. Determine if your project is high volume, low volume, high customization, or low customization. Probably the biggest shortfall in pricing is not being fairly compensated for your time. There will be time in meetings, time designing framing, time preparing proposals and revisions, time at job sites, time at installations, driving time, and parking. Consequently, all of these time-consuming activities need to be factored in when considering pricing. A formula with the cost of materials may be a good way to price out the framing portion of the job. If you have a retail pricing schedule for framing, you can use it as a benchmark to compare what the actual retail value of each framed piece would be.

The bottom line is to be competitive and at the same time take into account what your time is worth and set your price accordingly. Your time has value. Naturally, the more experience you gain, the more valuable your time will become. Do not fall into a pattern of giving your time away. Some consultants prefer to charge an hourly rate, while others will factor in their time with the entire proposal. If you are not charging an hourly rate, the cost of the job needs to compensate for the coordination and administrative costs for shipping, meetings, design time, proposal writing, and other related activities. Keep a mileage log in your car and record the mileage to business meetings and job sites. Mileage is a tax-deductible expense.

Once you have your pricing finalized, prepare a detailed proposal outlining the job specifications and your terms. I tend to leave off the artist's name and list the piece by description. For example, I will list a piece as photograph of seawall. This way it is more difficult for the decision maker to email my proposal to a competitor and match the artwork and framing specifications. I list a description of the frame, but I do not list a supplier's name. Unfortunately, with the ease of electronic communications, I learned from experience not to list too much detail. I found out the hard way that some of my proposals were sent to competitors with the intention of being copied. Larger jobs may require artists to be listed, in which case I comply.

Make a conscious effort to prepare your proposals and quotations as soon as possible after your final meeting. This shows you are a serious contender and want the business. Most importantly, if you tell your client you will have the proposal on a certain date, follow through. I was bidding on a healthcare clinic and was told by the architect to have my proposal in on a certain date. He informed me that he was considering two other art consultants. I had my proposal in a day early. When I was able to reach him on the phone to confirm he had received my proposal, he proceeded to tell me neither of the other consultants had submitted their proposals on time. He awarded the contract to me without even looking at the other proposals. The difference between me and the other consultants was my eagerness to show competency and professionalism coupled with a great selection of artists and competitive pricing.

Contact your prospect within 24 hours to confirm the quotation or proposal has been received. Ask if he/she has any questions and when a decision will be made. Should any revisions need to be made, do so promptly. Moreover, if your proposal is rejected, find out why and use the process as a learning experience. Remember, there is a learning curve. Even if you did not get the job, that person may use you in the future. In my experience, it has paid off to wait patiently on the sidelines and be available when a competitor fails to perform. Being number two has served me well and has allowed me to secure the number one position when a competitor failed. I have also been awarded contracts with companies who have grown tired of their consultants complaining that everything looks the same from job to job. A company that once told me "no" was suddenly receptive to having me work with them. Keep in contact with companies that have rejected you because there will always be more jobs in the future.

Keep in mind that corporate art sales are built on relationships that are based on integrity, trust, value, quality, and professionalism. Never express disappointment or negativity to a prospect who chooses a competitor. Avoid the temptation to say anything negative about one of your competitors. Keep the door open for future opportunities. Sometimes you will not be awarded a contract for uncontrollable reasons. It is not always about price. The consultant may have been selected because they have a personal connection with the decision maker. Unfortunately, in this business, sometimes the consultant awarded a contract is not necessarily the best qualified. A combination of timing, luck, professionalism, persistence, and connections helps you win contracts.

Requests for Qualifications, Requests for Proposals, and Call for Artists

When an institution plans a new facility and needs an art consultant on board, a Request for Qualifications (RFQ) or a Request for Proposal (RFP) is written and distributed. The difference between these two documents is that with a RFQ the objective is to find qualified professionals to consider for a project, and with a RFP the candidate is prequalified and must submit their proposed concept for a project.

Art consultants may be on both sides of the spectrum when it comes to a RFQ. Writing a RFQ is a tedious process but one that is necessary when working on a large project where the art consultant's role is to find artists for the project. Art consultants working in this capacity are under a negotiated contract and are paid to perform services such as writing RFQs and contracts for artists. These written preparations may not be something all art consultants want to take on, but knowing what these terms are all about is very important. Most seasoned art consultants will both write RFQs and make submissions for these types of large projects. RFQ and RFP are regular terms that art consultants use in daily business. Responding to a RFQ in hopes of winning a contract to provide art advisement services is a process all art consultants should welcome at some time in their careers.

With a RFQ, a bid solicitation detailing the scope of the project is sent via email to prospective candidates with the objective of finding qualified art consultants within a geographic area. For example, the state of California may need an art consultant for a healthcare facility in Los Angeles. A RFQ is sent with guidelines for completion within a certain time frame, and in order to qualify, the candidates may be required to live within 100 miles of Los Angeles. The solicitation will have a bid number, bid title, bid start date, bid end date, and standard disclaimer. A website is listed for amendments to bid documents and bid solicitations with the understanding that bidders are responsible for checking to see if any changes in the solicitation have been made.

An art consultant considering a RFQ should expect to review a lengthy document that outlines the project and lists specific questions to be answered. Standard language in the document states the institution does not discriminate by using race, religion, sex, ethnicity, or national origin as criteria to award contracts. Consultants must confirm no conflict of interest as specified in the document. Qualification packets must be received by the deadline stated, and multiple copies are usually required both electronically and in print. Questions focus on prior work experience, client relationships, scheduling, production capabilities, and problem solving. Citing examples of relevant situations exemplifying success at project management, the applicant needs to make a convincing argument that he/she is qualified to take on the proposed project.

Applicants are required to list a team of three or four qualified support staff and identify their roles. Each team member must include a current resume. While these requirements may eliminate independent art consultants working out of their homes, consultants having larger businesses seek these types of opportunities. Contracts can be for several years with options for renewal. Long terms projects are challenging and can be quite lucrative. Having a few of these jobs under your belt will be advantageous when being considered for other large and demanding types of projects.

In completing a RFQ, professional references are also required. It is optional to supply a client list and supplemental material such as brochures or published articles. While it is best to streamline and succinctly answer each question, the inclusion of additional support material may mean the difference between getting an interview or not being considered at all. The RFQ will specify when applicants will receive notice if they are being considered for hire.

A Request for Proposal (RFP) is a more detailed document to complete, because the art consultant is required to select the artwork, propose a concept, specify art locations, choose framing materials, and address any other considerations for the project. Essentially you are proposing a master art plan for the project. Similarly to a RFQ, the consultant lists references and team members with identifying roles. Local jobs require the consultant to make a presentation showing artwork and framing selections. Electronic submissions include visuals of the artwork and art locations.

For example, if the RFP is for a law firm, the art consultant would select appropriate artwork and express how the artwork would reinforce the strong corporate image of the firm. The submission would address all of the requirements as outlined in the RFP. The more RFPs an art consultant submits, the easier the process becomes. Decision makers reviewing RFPs are made up of committee members with experience and a high regard for professionalism. After reviewing the candidate's submissions, the committee will develop a short list of applicants to be interviewed. It may be a daunting and nerve-wracking process to compete for these types of jobs. Often due to construction delays, decisions are postponed and the uncertainty can be stressful. Ideally, it is best not to count on being awarded contracts, and if it happens it is a welcome surprise.

The following are criteria used to select top art consultants submitting for a RFP:
1. Ability to develop a master art plan and provide a vision for the facility.
2. Ability to develop artist's proposals in seeking regional artists for review by an art advisory committee.
3. Ability to review submissions by artists and determine feasibility and compatibility of commissioned artists to specific areas of the facility.
4. Ability to coordinate art commissions and oversee fabrications and installations.
5. Ability to write proposals for review of team members including architects, engineers, project managers, and interior designers.
6. Ability to work with potential art donors.
7. Ability to provide art budgets and schedules.
8. Ability to develop contracts specifically between artists and the institution.
9. Ability to coordinate each phase of the project within budget and on time.

The following are criteria used for art consultants writing a RFQ in seeking artists for a large project. The role of the art consultant is to find interested artists with these qualifications:
1. Prior experience working as a team member with architects, project managers, engineers, and interior designers.
2. Ability to provide creative, innovative, and technically sound artwork with a high level of craftsmanship.
3 Aptitude for presenting ideas, meeting budgets, and interpreting project requirements.
4 Strength of resume outlining previous art solutions for public art.
5 Positive attitude and personal interest in the success of the project.
6 Ability to meet deadlines.
7 Quality and strength of artistic vision. Presenting fresh ideas not derivative of other artistic styles.
8 Competency in electronic communication.

Chapter 8

Closing Sales and Maintaining Client Relationships

Purchasing artwork is different from most purchases a business will make. You can sense an emotional connection when you show exciting artwork to buyers. Capitalize on that excitement and articulate why the piece or pieces of artwork are perfect for the space. The key is to listen to what your client is saying. Do less talking and more listening and you will hear the cues. Clients will give you cues when they are ready to close a sale. Corporations often have opening parties or need projects completed by a certain time. This information may be mentioned at the meeting and is a good way to close a sale.

Closing sales is a learned skill that takes time and practice to develop. With art consulting not only are you selling yourself, but you are selling the artwork and solutions. Missed opportunities for closing sales may be the direct result of weak or unsuitable art offerings compared to what a competitor may have presented. To close sales as an art consultant you will need to present yourself as a confident expert who can handle all aspects of the art program.

Questions from your prospects to signal cues when they may be ready to close a sale:
1. When can you have this order completed by? Can you have it for our opening event?
2. Do you need a deposit to get started?
3. Can we design the frames for these pieces?
4. What is the quickest turnaround time you can give me?
5. Are your installers available on the date I need these pieces hung?
6. Can you get the proposal to me as soon as possible?
7. Does your company take credit cards?

An experienced art consultant will develop a strategy to capture and keep repeat business with companies that continue to expand. The fields of healthcare and hospitality may be the best bets in finding clients who will provide ongoing business. Remember to balance your time between seeking new clients and maintaining business with your loyal clients.

Communicate with your contacts and nurture the business relationship. As with any personal relationship, show interest and let your client know you are always there to service the account. One of the best ways to build relationships is to ask questions about your client's family, travel experiences, and interests. Keep this information in your computer and review it before initiating a conversation. The fact that you remember their spouse's name, children's name, travels, and interests helps establish a closeness and shows you are a caring individual. Clients will respond positively with surprise and admiration when you show a personal interest in their activities outside of the workplace. This is another strategy to set yourself apart from your competition. Remember, clients will buy from sales people they like, trust, and consider business friends. Gathering personal information and using it in conversations will allow you to establish a deeper and more solid relationship. The key is to keep track of personal information and refer to it at opportune times. Having a great memory also helps tremendously.

Once a business friendship has been established, repeat business and referrals will follow. In many cases the business friendship will be so strong, your client will not even consider doing business with one of your competitors. However, never take these business relationships for granted. Communicate often and continue to give excellent value and service. Send holiday cards and hand-written thank you notes to show your appreciation. Invite these clients to net-working events as your guests. Make them feel special and thank them often for using your services.

Constant communication with your clients will help you forecast the next three to six months with upcoming projects, allowing you to fill in the slow times with prospecting for new clients. Routine communication with your established business contacts will also alert you of possible changes in the company, giving you time to develop ways to maintain the account if your contact leaves.

Trickle down business

The corporate environment opens up an excellent networking opportunity to create more business by internal referrals and word of mouth. By working on a corporate project, you are introduced to a new, captive audience. Here are some valuable tips to capitalize on ways to add more art and framing sales when working with a corporation:

1. Get to know as many company employees as possible and distribute your business cards.
2. Suggest framing diplomas, certificates, postings, bulletin boards, and mirrors.
3. Discuss adding pieces for individual offices not included in the budget. When possible ask the facilities manager to send an email to the staff about your company and the services you offer.
4. Visit the job site after completion and inquire about referrals or any additional pieces needed.
5. Leave extra business cards with the receptionist or facilities manager.
6. Send hand-written thank you notes.
7. Attend opening parties and receptions held at the corporations.
8. Attend holiday parties held at your client's offices.
9. Send holiday cards with a personalized note.

Intuition and practice will help you gain a better understanding of how to close sales and maintain client relationships. Business relationships are quite similar to personal friendships. By applying the same principles of constant communication and asking questions about personal interests and family happenings, you can solidify business relationships. As your business grows, your loyal clients will follow. Take the necessary steps to keep these clients happy and you will reap the benefits over and over again. There is much truth to the business principle that it is easier to maintain relationships with loyal clients than to go out and find new clients. It all comes down to the philosophy that business people prefer to do business with friends.

Chapter 9

Framing

Learning the basics of custom picture framing is a necessity for all art consultants. Whether or not your company does in house custom picture framing or you subcontract framing to a contract framer, framing design is part of the complete package you will be selling as a consultant. You will need to familiarize yourself with types of glazing, matting, and mouldings. Corporate artwork has a distinct framing style. It differs from residential framing. Without a good working knowledge of framing design, you will be at a big disadvantage when getting to the framing phase of the art program. Having inspiring and strong artwork may win you a contract, but if you cannot pull the elements of frame design together to showcase the artwork and blend in with the corporate environment, you are doing your client a disservice. Innovative framing design sets off the artwork.

Unfortunately, mediocre framing is often seen in corporate environments because art consultants or interior designers do not have a deep understanding of framing design. With the advent of giclees printed on canvas, many design professionals are using gallery wrapped pieces in lieu of framed artwork. While gallery wrapped canvas pieces do have their place, an entire art program of gallery wraps is uninspiring. From experience, I advise getting to know all you can about picture framing. It will set you apart from your competition and showcase your artwork. Classes on picture framing are taught at the West Coast Art and Frame Show held in Las Vegas every January. If you are serious about becoming a corporate art consultant, attend this conference at least once to take picture framing classes and meet art and framing suppliers.

Since custom framing is expensive, some consultants tend to specify under-scale frames to save money. Inferior quality of acrylic is often specified. Nonarchival paper mats that are not acid-free are put on fine art to lower costs. Art consultants need to educate their clients about good framing design. Do not skimp on materials. In the course of my career, I have won many contracts with decision makers who have used art consultants before me specifying cheap or dull framing design. Consequently, our company has had to redo inferior framing with bowing acrylic or frames coming apart because they were poorly constructed or not strong enough. Did the company really save any money if the pieces had to be reframed after a few years? It is imperative that you attempt to educate the decision makers and compare "apples to apples" when specifying framing materials in a proposal.

The purpose of writing about framing is not to teach you how to frame, but instead to help you grasp the importance of good framing design. Why perpetuate mediocre framing? Naturally, having the whole package of impressive art and well-designed framing will most likely win you more contracts. When I see mediocre framing, it sparks a competitive chord within me to educate decision makers about framing during my presentations. This is one area where an art consultant can differentiate themselves from their competition. All custom picture framing is not created equal. Art consultants need to consistently specify appropriate materials and substantiate their choices when meeting with clients. Under designing and under engineering framing will cause one to lose credibility over the course of time. Equally important, overselling jobs by specifying overpriced materials is just as bad as under selling. The key is to take the time to learn how to sell proper framing and educate your client in the process of closing the sale.

Why is picture framing perceived as expensive?

Picture framing is one of the last surviving custom businesses where a customer can select from a large number of frames and matting materials to custom create a design specific to their size and taste. One custom-created piece can be made to order; there is no minimum number of pieces required. The selections of materials are vast. Similarly, tailors custom fabricate suits, hand selecting fabrics and fitting everything to the client's personal measurements.

Picture framing cannot take place in a small location. Equipment and apparatus such as computerized mat cutters, metal and wood saws, wall cutters for glass, spray booths, under-pinning machines, mounting presses, air filtering systems, etc. take up a lot of space and are expensive to purchase and maintain. In addition, worktables, design counters, walls for frame samples, and storage space are all needed. Picture framing is labor intensive because each piece is handmade. Overhead and labor costs are high.

Trained picture framers work diligently with a heightened sense of detail to ensure each piece is executed to the client's specifications and with the highest level of craftsmanship. Picture framers possess the proper skills to handle and care for artwork from inexpensive posters to high-end investment quality artwork. The techniques and skills picture framers master include building frames, stretching and blocking canvasses, hand wrapping fabric mats, applying gold leaf finishes, sewing, making fabric platforms, and installing artwork. The point is that picture framers do not make minimum wage, and they do more than simply clean glass and put art into frames.

Certified Picture Framers (CPF Exam)

In 1986, the Professional Picture Framers Association (PPFA) developed the CPF exam to test picture framers and picture framing designers on a large body of knowledge pertaining to the industry. Individuals passing the CPF exam have demonstrated technical efficiency in the preservation and framing techniques of works on paper, canvas, textiles, as well as three-dimensional objects. The purpose of the CPF exam is to benchmark the industry standards and recognize picture framers' levels of competency in the areas of preservation, general knowledge, math, mechanics, and mounting. Art consultants bringing their artwork to a picture framing businesses operating under the direction of certified pictured framers may rest assured the framing will be done right. The PPFA has also recently administered a MCPF exam (Master Certified Picture Framer) as part of the continuing education program for the industry.

Art consultants interviewing contract framers to form a business relationship should question their credentials. The following are questions to consider when interviewing a framing company:

1. How many picture framers are on staff and how many are certified?
2. What kind of turnaround times may be expected?
3. Do they offer installation services?

4. How do their prices compare with other framers in the area?
5. Do they have the ability to store large projects?
6. Do they have the necessary equipment to handle production framing?
7. Can they juggle several large jobs at one time?
8. How long have they been in business?
9. Can they work on large pieces and specialized designs?
10. Can they build crates?
11. What is their policy regarding damaged artwork while being framed?
12. What kind of insurance do they carry?

All framing designs for clients should be kept on file for future reference. Often corporate clients will want to duplicate existing framing designs at a later date. The ability to retrieve this information is very important. Not only does it save time to have the designs specifications at your fingertips, but also it shows excellent customer service and competency. If a client requests the same mat colors and frame used three years ago, you should be able to duplicate the design unless the frame has been discontinued. Implement a system to retrieve this information either electronically or by storing work orders in binders for easy access. Equally important is the ability to look up the artist and title of each piece purchased. For example, if a client had purchased 100 framed posters several years ago and wants to add another group of posters for an expanded area of the building, in order to not repeat prior images you will need to have records detailing each piece purchased. Also, having a record of the type of glazing and mat dimensions is vital.

Rules and guidelines for framing corporate artwork:

1. Do not skimp on materials. Use archival mats on fine art.
2. Use a high-grade acrylic with a minimum of .118 thickness.
3. Finish off the back of the frame with a dust cover.
4. Use a frame that visually balances the scale of the design. Do not use under scale frames to save money.
5. Use ultraviolet filtering glass unless there is a safety issue.
6. Use acrylic glazing in hospitals and on oversize pieces.
7. Vary mat proportions according to the size of the artwork.
8. Avoid nonglare glass on matted pieces.
9. Do not put glazing directly against fine art without matting or use of spacers.
10. Do not mount fine art. Hinge it.
11. Do not trim fine art without permission from the artist.
12. Show the artist's signature on fine art; do not mat over it.
13. Do not leave artwork (framed or unframed) in a car for an extended period of time.
14. Protect framed artwork with cardboard corners and other packaging materials.
15. Keep good records of framing materials for future reference.

As a general rule, frames selected for the corporate environment match or blend with the furniture and overall look of the space. For example, when the casework is done in walnut, most likely a walnut colored wood frame or a frame that blends with the furniture will be used. Matting is selected to blend with fabrics, wall treatments, and floors. While metal sectional frames were popular in the 1980s and 1990s, wood frames are predominately used in corporate settings today. Framing should not distract the viewer from seeing the artwork. Neutral top mats will bring the viewer's eye into the artwork.

By contrast, using brightly colored top mats such as primary colors, will detract from the artwork and draw undue attention to the frame design. To add visual interest and provide a more upscale look, the frames on fine art pieces may differ from the framing of posters when designing a job requiring each type of artwork. Wood frames with metallic washes look stunning on fine art in corporate spaces, often blending with travertine floors, tile, and wallpaper. Another way to differentiate the framing of fine art and poster art is to use 8-ply mats or linen mats on fine art and 4-ply paper mats on posters. Successful framing design will present the art program as a flowing collection of pieces complementary to the architectural features and design style of the space.

Art consultants work closely with moulding representatives to keep abreast of the current contract mouldings available. As mouldings are discontinued, corner samples are discarded. When a consultant is proposing a large job, checking stock on the moulding is crucial. If possible, try to hold the amount of footage needed in anticipation of closing the job. Often, with repeat corporate clients, you will not be bidding against a competitor, and you can be confident the job will close. Many picture framing representatives will reserve the moulding while you wait to receive your purchase order. A good relationship with your moulding representative may mean the difference between getting the materials you need to complete the job or having to redesign. You do not want to be caught short of footage required to complete a job or worse yet, have the moulding be unavailable when you are ready to proceed with an order.

A competent art consultant will know not only how to sell artwork but how to frame it cost effectively, without compromising good design. Having the skill set to sell both art and framing will help you succeed. A common mistake art consultants make is to downplay the framing part of an art program. I have won many contracts with decision makers due to the fact that I had the ability to educate my clients about framing and step it up from what a previous consultant had sold them. Take the time to study and learn about picture framing because it is an integral part of the whole package. Again, this is another way you can set yourself apart from your competition.

Do not rely solely on a contract framer to design the framing portion of your art program. Even if you opt to outsource framing, learn all you can about framing materials and have your own corner samples. Meet and form relationships with picture framing representatives. Learn about framing techniques and the proper ways to frame artwork. Should your client ask about the difference between conservation clear glass and museum glass, be educated enough to give a correct answer. Be prepared to discuss archival treatments, glazing options, mounting methods, oversize matting, floating, and other common framing terms. If your competition is discussing these aspects of framing and you are not, who has the advantage? Every little edge you have over your competitors will help you win contracts. Learn all you can about framing.

Chapter 10

Installations

Corporate decision makers rely on art consultants to take charge of art installations. Before the artwork is delivered to a job site for installation, the consultant should have predetermined the art placement and specified whether or not it is a security installation. Sometimes art consultants will need to deviate from their original art placement plan, but in most cases it should be followed. A number of unusual circumstances can arise such as curved walls, concrete and brick walls, or hanging on an atrium wall requiring a scaffold. Art consultants need to be educated about all types of installations and discuss the best solutions with their clients before submitting a proposal. Our company notes the kind of installation on the framing work order, dictating the necessary hanging hardware to be attached to the back of the artwork. This is a time-saving measure and makes our installations run very smoothly.

There are two types of installations that will make up the majority of routine installations. These are security installations and double strap installations. Healthcare facilities and banks usually require security installations. Artwork placed in hotels and lobbies of corporate buildings also generally opt for security installations. The majority of other corporate artwork is hung on a double strap hanging system. In both kinds of systems, the art is hung with a level and will always hang straight. This is especially important when hanging a series of pieces. Hanging from wire will not achieve the same results. With wire the artwork will shift around, therefore it is inefficient and not precise.

The double strap hanging system uses two single hole "D-ring" hangers on each side of the back of the frame. D-rings come in sizes to accommodate either a 30-pound hanger or a 50-pound hanger. Most often we use the larger D-rings with a 50-pound hanger (instead of a 30-pound hanger) which adds a bit more strength to the installation. If the installer hits a metal stud, the nail will usually penetrate the stud without bending. To simplify and speed up installation, our framers always install the D-rings the same distance down from the top of the frame. A measurement marking the distance between the holes of the D-rings is written on the back of the frame. When installing multiple same sized pieces, the installation goes very quickly because the distance down from the top of all pieces is fixed, making the distance apart easy to calculate.

For security installations, a component system is used with two brackets at the top and a "T-lock" at the bottom. It saves time at the installation when the hardware is attached to the back of the frame while the artwork is in the frame shop. The mating hardware is attached to the wall where the piece is to be installed. Another time-saving measure is to install the brackets the same difference in from the outside of the frame. The distance between the centers should be measured and written on the back of the dust cover. This way, when the frame is installed, the holes for the top brackets will always be the same distance down from the top of the frame and the same distance in from the edges. Installation will be precise, as the holes are always a known distance from the top and sides.

Other types of installations that an art consultant may encounter, especially when selling mirrors for a hospitality job, use a cleat system. When the goal is to have the mirror or artwork hang as closely to the wall as possible, a Z-type channel is used. This system uses two interlocking pieces of aluminum. One piece is attached to the wall and the other is attached to the back of the frame. Similarly, a wood cleat system is used to hang large acrylic boxes with wood strainers. When installed, the piece hangs perfectly flat to the wall because the cleat is recessed inside the frame and is part of the strainer.

In corporate spaces where entrances have especially high ceilings, a scaffold may be necessary in order to hang the artwork at the right height. Planning for the rental of trucks, scaffolds, and scissor lifts should be considered in advance of the installation date. Having a fully equipped installation kit is also essential when unexpected situations occur. Sometimes clients will request installations for artwork that has not been seen, and what the client describes is not always what needs to be done. This means having back up tools and hardware ready to problem solve.

Installations are time consuming and should be charged accordingly. Art consultants may charge an hourly rate for installations or factor it in as part of the whole package. Preferably, charge an hourly rate, and consider the cost of the hardware as well. Invariably decision makers assisting you with installations are pulled in many directions and much time is wasted in getting their attention and approval. Project managers in medical facilities want to confirm the art placements before an installer makes a hole in the newly painted or wallpapered wall. If the job has been priced installed, there is a chance that it will take longer than expected. For your protection, put a clause in the proposal stating return trips will be an additional charge. For example, when our installers were at one health clinic, an entire suite had defective wallpaper and consequently the installation required a return trip. Since the proposal stated return trips would be billed separately, our time was compensated.

Installation rates vary per company. Charges usually range from $60 to $120 per hour for a one-man crew and $75 to $200 per hour for a two-man crew. With high fuel costs, some companies charge a trip fee. Consider charging for driving time, especially for long distances and expected traffic delays. It is tricky to estimate how much time an installation will take. By including clauses in the proposal stating the actual time of the installation will be billed, the art consultant is better off than if he/she guesses and underestimates the time. This way you can bill your client for additional installation time after the installation has been completed.

To speed up the installation, create a labeling system. For example, in a hospital, identify the floor, east or west wing, and write this information along with a piece number on the back of the artwork. When unloading, have the artwork separated according to where it will be hung. Invest in several large rolling carts to move the artwork around. Bring your blueprints or floor plans to the job site to expedite art placement. Count the pieces as they are placed and have a check and balance system. These extra steps will save time and help the installation run smoother.

How does an art consultant know the height and position of the pieces to be installed? It comes with experience. For the novice consultant, try visiting new buildings such as hospitals and hotels and study the art and how it is hung. Part of it is intuition and looking at how the artwork balances with the furniture and surroundings. Experience is the best teacher. There is no real formula to follow. Art consultants need to develop this skill and be confident in making the right decisions at installations. Remember, the art consultant is the expert and directs the installation.

While at an installation, be polite and friendly to all employees. Always have business cards handy in case someone asks you for one. Notify staff that there will be some noise due to drilling and hammering. Be tidy and clean up all debris as you go along with either a small vacuum or a whisk broom and dust pan. With security installations, offer to leave a security wrench with the facilities manager in case the artwork needs to be removed at a future date and demonstrate how the security wrench is used.

Installation services are a significant part of the package when closing deals with clients. Rarely do corporate clients want to bother with hanging their own artwork. Become familiar with all types of installations and educate your client. If you are an independent art consultant, work closely with a professional installer who can accommodate your clients' needs. When your client inquires about earthquake safety, theft protection, hanging on a curved or brick wall, mirror installations, or hanging a series of pieces, make sure you are knowledgeable and can give them the correct information.

Call 24 hours ahead to confirm installations. Show up for an installation on time and be helpful. If a client asks you to hang a bulletin board or their existing artwork, be agreeable and offer to hang it and anything else they need installed. Once the installation is complete, do a walk through with the contact person to look at each piece. Get feedback, and once the contact person has approved the installation, get a signature on the delivery receipt. It is very important to show proof of receipt of the goods when trying to get paid for a job.

Installations are the last phase of a job cycle. Capitalize on the opportunity to thank your client for using your services. Bring a digital camera and take pictures. Drop off business cards with the receptionist and your contact person. Most importantly, leave on a friendly note and follow up with a handwritten thank you note. If the client seems responsive and willing, ask for a letter of recommendation. Keep in contact and remember, repeat business is easier to perpetuate than going after new business.

Chapter 11

Getting Paid

In a perfect world, deposit checks and balance due checks will flow through your business on time. Unfortunately, getting paid is not always easy and can take hours of extra time. In proposals you may state your terms require a 50% deposit to proceed, with the balance either COD (cash on delivery) or NET 30. For new clients and some corporate clients these terms are fine. However, with large institutions it is sometimes more difficult to get a deposit on jobs under $10,000. Purchase orders from these larger institutions are generally issued stating the terms as NET 30 from the date of delivery or installation. Collecting payment requires proof of delivery and repeated follow up with phone calls and emails. While construction time lines dictate art installations, other departments handling funding may halt payment for various reasons. The person who needs to sign off on a check may be sick, on vacation, or overworked. Often finding the people in the accounting department can be time consuming and difficult. Once you locate the right person, half the battle is behind you. Always be polite when speaking on the phone or sending email communications in your quest for payment.

Often with large institutions, several people will need to approve payment. Documents go from project managers, to their bosses, through other channels, and finally to the accounting department. It takes time for each person to review the paperwork required for payment. Once the payment has been approved, it takes additional time to get the check processed. Check runs may be scheduled every other week causing further delays. When at all possible, find out if payment has been approved and when the check will be mailed. If the check has not been approved, ask why and find out what the holdup is with your payment. Reasons for delays vary, but you can move the process along by keeping on top of the situation with constant communication. Being proactive is time consuming, but necessary to keep money flowing through your company.

Tips on getting paid
1. If the terms are COD, call 24 hours prior to the scheduled installation and confirm a check or credit card payment will be ready.
2. Accept all credit cards. Prepare a credit card authorization form to fax or email in anticipation of payment.
3. State in your proposal a 50% deposit is required to proceed with the order, and the turnaround time will be calculated from the date a deposit is received. Also state that the balance will be due upon delivery or installation. With larger institutions, you will need to follow their protocol for the terms and payment schedules.
4. Document all communication you have with the corporation's accounting department.
5. Follow up with phone calls and emails to inquire about reasons for delay.
6. Present delivery receipts for signature at all deliveries and installations to document proof of delivery and job completion.

7. Send a copy of the signed delivery receipt with all invoices.
8. Always be polite with your contact at the accounting department.
9. Inquire about check cutting and mailing cycles.
10. Do not be reluctant to investigate why payments are delayed. Many times invoices are misplaced.
11. Ask the check number when you have been notified a check has been issued. If you do not receive the check on the date promised, call the following day and ask what happened. Identify the check number when inquiring about the status of payment.
12. Be persistent.
13. Keep a list of contacts at all accounting departments you are dealing with. These contacts will come in handy in the future with repeat business. If a company is late with payment, there is a good chance it will be late again with another order.

Chapter 12

Working With Artists

Finding artists

I describe the stable of artists an art consultant has as their ammunition to close a sale. The more artists you have unique to your business, the more capable you will appear. It is imperative that each art program you complete does not look the same. The overall design needs to be fresh, and the way to keep projects jobs looking fresh is to use different and exciting artists on each job. Finding artists that your competitors do not have is critical. Also knowing what type of artists will sell and be of interest to your clients is very important. There is a plethora of ways to find new artists, but if you do not know what type of artists will best suit your client's taste, you may be wasting valuable time. Artwork styles change with trends in architecture and interior design. Color palettes also change, and what may have sold in 1990 most likely will look dated in 2015. It is the art consultant's responsibility to maintain artist relationships and constantly find new artists. In order to stand out from your competition, you need to have interesting artists and a large variety of artists in many price ranges.

Art consultants need to continually search for new artists and add to their stable of artists. This is not to say each artist relationship has to be an exclusive arrangement or that art publishers may not be considered as sources. The more sources you have at your fingertips, the easier it will be to match artists and art with potential clients. Remember, you are entering into a client relationship as the expert. You need to have a considerable number of sources and present a strong package to all of your clients. This means finding artists who do all kinds of artwork from photography, collage, giclees on paper, original canvas, and ceramics to wall sculptures, free-standing sculptures, and more. An art consultant can never have enough artists to show, and one of the biggest mistakes a consultant makes is to use the same artists over and over. Remember, each art program needs to look fresh and not a repeat of what was done on a previous project. For example, I recently began working with a new client, and one of the first things discussed was not using any of the artists I had placed in a business that was a main competitor of theirs. This was not problematic for me since I had a large stable of artists to show my new client without repeating ones I had sold to the competing business. Interestingly enough, both clients had very similar tastes in art, but their jobs looked completely different with no overlap of artists selected.

In order to know what kind of artists to work with, it is imperative that you visit several corporate spaces to see what type of artwork has been purchased. Visit new buildings and take notice of the public artwork specified in terms of color, size, media, art placement, and subject matter. Naturally, if you are unfamiliar with the look of corporate artwork you will not be able to sell it. So step one is to become familiar with the corporate look. Visit newly opened banks, restaurants, hotels, hospitals, medical clinics, law firms, Class A buildings, and retirement facilities to look at the artwork and framing. I still continue to go into new spaces to see what kind of artwork has been specified and ponder about what I would have done had I been hired. Generally speaking, you will see landscapes, abstracts, or three-dimensional pieces in the buildings you have visited. Also take notice of what you do not see which will most likely be figurative pieces, folk art, surreal art, and art with colors that do not blend with the environment such as bright purple or too much black.

Once you have familiarized yourself with the look of corporate artwork, you are ready to spend time finding artists and sources. An excellent starting point is to attend the West Coast Art and Frame Show held annually for the art and framing industry. At the trade show conference you will find art publishers and some artists who will be perfect for your clients. However, this is only a starting point, because almost everyone in the art and framing industry will have access to the same sources. What will set you apart from your competition is having a large selection of unique artists. But how do you find these artists?

No doubt it is time consuming to find new artists, but the information technology of today has made it much easier than it used to be. Most serious artists have websites, and it is fairly easy to find them. When I started looking for artists in the 1980s, it was much more difficult. I had to rely on putting ads in art magazines or finding artists through my travels. Every year I had to review hundreds of slides and return the rejected slides in a self-addressed stamped envelope. Now, with the click of a mouse I can check out an artist's website and at least have a pretty good idea of artist compatibility with my business. Many artists put links on their website to other artists that are worth investigating.

One way of finding artists is to look in poster art catalogs. Art consultants definitely will need to acquire poster art catalogs, considering many jobs require a combination of fine art and poster art. I have found several artists by contacting them after seeing their work published in poster art catalogs. Also, there are many local artist websites specific to where you live. In San Diego, we have the San Diego Visual Arts Network, which is an excellent way to meet new artists. Find out what artist organizations are particular to where you live.

Another creative way to find artists is to trade information with a gallery owner outside of your geographic area. If you have a good selling artist, you can trade that information with a gallery owner for exchange of a source for you. I make a conscious effort to get to know other art consultants nationwide for the purpose of trading information about artists and ideas about growing our respective businesses. Artists can also introduce you to a gallery in another city. Checking out websites of galleries can spark your interest in particular artists. Do not assume artists may not be interested in working with you just because you are starting out. It never hurts to contact an artist and inquire about being represented. Posting a notice on your website that you are looking for new artists will stir up interest.

I have also found several wonderful artists through my associations with networking groups. One of my best selling artists is the spouse of a networking business friend. He does wonderful photographic scenes of San Diego, and since many of my corporate clients request local San Diego images, his work is very popular. I also ask my artists if they know of any artists who may be interested in working with me. I have found artists through other artists I might meet in my travels. I have discovered wonderful artists by attending local art festivals. One other excellent way to find artists is through social networking sites such as LinkedIn. Recently, I found two artists through an artist group on LinkedIn. The beauty of LinkedIn is that once you find one artist it leads to a whole new network of artists who know each other. The Guild.com is also a great source for locating artists.

To review, you can find artists:
1. Attending art festivals
2. Investigating local artist organizations
3. Networking groups
4. Exchanging information with other gallery owners
5. Looking at poster catalogs
6. Attending trade shows such as the West Coast Art and Frame Show
7. Visiting galleries when traveling
8. Posting inquiries on your website
9. Social networking sites such as LinkedIn
10. Looking at websites of artists and other galleries
11. Asking your artists for introductions to artists they know
12. The Guild.com

Support materials, agreements, and working with your artists

Art consultants generally work differently with artists than gallery owners do. Since the main objective is to place artwork in a corporate setting and not to promote the artist through gallery openings, art consultants need agreements in writing and support materials provided by the artists. Agreements specify the works on consignment, the NET price to the artist, the length of time the artwork will be consigned, and who pays for shipping. In most cases, I ask my artist to pay for shipping to my business, and I pay for shipping back of unsold pieces. The agreement also states that I will insure the pieces while in my possession, and I will be responsible for items damaged. All artwork is inspected upon receipt, and if any damage has occurred in shipping it is noted and dealt with immediately. Examine the artwork in raking light.

Whether or not you decide to oversee commissions or focus on orchestrating projects that require sending artwork back and forth, it is necessary to have forms outlining your agreements with artists. Being organized and keeping good records will save you time. Have a policy in writing about payments to your artists. Find out if your artists take credit cards. Put the terms in writing such as shipping costs and payment terms. Being upfront about payment schedules will ease stress and help eliminate calls from artists about when they will get paid.

When writing an artist agreement, consider the following points:
1. Put everything in writing.
2 List each piece on the consignment form and the NET price to the artist.
3. List the duration of the agreement.
4. Do not leave pieces at a third party unless you have permission from the artist.
5. Have an agreement in writing about payment schedules.
6. Agree on shipping costs and insuring artwork in transit.
7. Adjust consignment forms immediately when pieces are sold or returned.
8. Consult with an attorney when composing a commission agreement for the first time.
9. Understand that the artist retains all copyrights to their works.

I request that my artists create binders with visuals of their work that I take to meetings with decision makers. These binders have photographic images of a wide range of their work, often showing commissions and including published articles. I cannot stress enough the extreme value each binder has in stirring the interest of viewers. Having binders of your artists is an efficient way to show a variety of artists in a short period of time and in turn learn what your client likes or dislikes. I tell artists who resist the idea of sending me binders that they will be at a disadvantage, because I will be bringing binders of other artists to my meetings. When I explain the reason behind creating a binder, my artists produce one for my library. They understand I need their binder as a sales tool. In addition to the binders, I usually keep 2 to 10 pieces of their work on consignment to show my clients.

When I have a specific project I am working on such as a medical facility or corporate office, I will contact my artists and ask them to send me additional pieces in a certain style, color palette, and size. I know from previous experience that I will need a good body of work to show the decision makers. Some of my artists I sell quite often and other artists may not sell at all. If I cannot sell an artist's work within one year, I will reassess the relationship and either return the artwork or give the artist some direction to create artwork that I feel I can sell.

Many artists send CDs of their work when I start a relationship with them. I use the CD to review their body of work and give them guidance about the pieces I think my clients would find favorable. Although I do not use their CDs in my presentations, I do find them useful to keep as a reference. All of my artists provide biographical information and current pricing information. Relationships evolve over time, and I correspond periodically through email to see what my artists are currently creating. Each artist relationship is unique with the common goal of selling artwork. I treat my artists fairly, with respect, and I pay them when work is sold.

As previously mentioned, I add new artists all the time and make it part of my routine to look for interesting artwork. Part of the process is educating artists about what I do and how we can work together. Since my company offers custom picture framing, I require all artwork sent to be unframed. I also coach artists on pricing and styles, giving them art direction. For example, I prefer to have a series of pieces that work together as a grouping rather than single pieces that stand alone. Artwork in a series can be placed down corridors, in conference rooms, and in other common areas. When doing an art plan, the pieces need to flow as a collection, therefore I advise my artists to have many compatible pieces and a body of work similar in style. Additionally, I guide them with color selections and subject matter.

I inform artists when and where their artwork is sold. When possible, I take photographs of their installed artwork and email them soon after the project has been completed. I invite local artists as my guests to opening parties and events held at facilities where I have sold their work. Not only do the artists get to see their artwork hanging in the building, but they enjoy participating in the opening celebration and meeting the design team. Inevitably, the design team is thrilled to meet the artist and the artist is thrilled to meet them. Artists take pride in seeing their work well framed and hanging in corporate settings.

When pieces are sold or returned, I make sure the original artist agreement is changed to note the disposition of the work. Keeping track of consigned work is not difficult, but it is imperative that any changes in the status of the artwork be changed immediately in writing. Going back after months and trying to reconstruct an art inventory of missing pieces is time consuming and shows a lack of respect to the artist. I do not lend out or leave consigned pieces to a third party. I do accommodate my client by emailing a visual or by leaving a color copy of a page from an artist's binder, but I do not leave artwork. My artists can rest assured that I know at all times where their artwork is and that it is in safe keeping.

I have many criteria to be considered when bringing on a new artist. What type of artwork do they offer? What are the price points? Does the work look unique? Will the artist do commissions? What other galleries or art consultants represent the artist? Can the art be rolled and shipped in a tube? Will the artist consign pieces? Is the artist professional? What kind of pricing structure will they offer me? I am surprised that some artists only give art consultants a 20% discount. I work on a 50/50 split with the majority of my artists. Some artists will not work with me unless I agree to buy their work out right. I decline. I have had artists whose work is overpriced, and I decline working with them as well. Over the years, I have developed a keen eye, and I know my market. If I am attracted to an artist's work but I cannot sell it, I will not start a relationship. For example, I rarely sell figurative artwork. An artist who does exquisite nude paintings may approach me, but knowing I cannot place that style of artwork, I would not work with that artist.

The types of artwork I sell most often to corporate buyers are giclees on paper and canvas, original paintings on paper, photographs, and mixed media pieces on paper. Subject matter differs from project to project, but generally a large selection of landscapes and abstracts will be where you want to concentrate your efforts when considering artwork for corporate clients. I represent artists who produce sculpture, three-dimensional wall pieces, works in glass, clay and metal, fiber pieces, mosaics, and wall murals. I keep files and information on artists who I have yet to contact, but may be a good fit for future projects. The artists I work with are not exclusive relationships by my choice. Understandably, I cannot promise performance to my artists because my jobs and projects vary from month to month. Essentially, I am hired to problem solve and show artists suitable for a particular corporate environment. How can I promote exclusive artists when each project presents a different set of parameters? My objective is to organize an art program with inspiring and exciting artwork that enhances the corporate environment while remaining sensitive to budget concerns. The methodology I use to find artists works for me, but each art consultant needs to create their own way of searching for and working with artists.

Regional versus non-regional artists

Art consultants searching for artists should consider representing both regional and non-regional artists. Since it is fairly easy to find local artists in the community, try to establish good working relationships with many of these artists in a variety of styles and mediums. Corporate decision makers tend to support local artists and often request specific scenes depicting local landmarks or landscapes. For example, in San Diego I repeatedly have corporate executives and project managers looking for local scenery of beaches, parks, neighborhoods, and landmarks. Quite often an entire project will be comprised of local San Diego photographic scenes, and I pride myself in having an extensive selection of San Diego imagery by my artists. Wherever you live, find local artists than can create recognizable scenes of your community. Corporations will seek out this type of artwork time and time again.

Of course not all of your local artists will create "community specific" artwork. Balance your selection of local artists creating artwork depicting local scenery with those who create everything else. Keep in mind that some corporate buyers will question you about which artists are local because their objective is to support local artists. In order to accommodate decision makers looking for local artists to support, have a large selection of them in your stable of artists. Again, this is an area where you can surpass your competition. If you do not have a broad selection of local artists and your competitors do, who has the advantage?

Artists residing in other parts of the country will add variety and richness to your stable of artists. The advantage of offering portfolios of artwork from non-regional artists is that your competition most likely will not have the same artists. Decision makers want to see variety and often inquire about where artists live. It looks impressive to have artists who reside in various parts of the country. Not only will the variety of artists captivate your audience, but sharing interesting biographical information and stories will help sell the artwork. Therefore, it is crucial to have a balance of outstanding local and non-local artists to show clients. Lastly, another point to consider that will undoubtedly occur often is that when showing interesting artwork, decision makers will request an appointment for residential consultation. Corporate art consultation leads to residential consultation, and the impetus is often the attraction of local portfolios of artwork. The key is to locate and show artists that will create a "wow" factor. Again the mix of local and non-local artists with an extensive selection of styles and price points will be a winning combination.

How artists find and work with art consultants

Artists realize that finding a good art consultant to sell their work may be an ideal setup. Given the fact that the majority of artists prefer to create artwork and not be involved in corporate art sales, the prospect of finding an art consultant that will show and sell their work is very appealing. Artists understand art consultants show a large variety of artwork by many artists to decision makers on a regular basis. It is highly unlikely that artists on their own would be able to make the kinds of appointments and connections art consultants can offer. In some cases, corporate buyers may purchase directly from an artist without an art consultant, but this does not happen often. Decision makers are quite busy and during an art presentation they want to see a full range of art possibilities, not just a portfolio from one artist.

Artists sometimes look to art consultants for pricing direction when determining the pricing structure of their work. Should an artist's retail pricing be unrealistic and perhaps out of line with fair market value, the consultant will advise the artist explaining budgetary concerns of corporations. Consultants have the knowledge to educate their artists about what subject matter sells, what sizes are the most common, what color palettes are current, and what price points are viable. Since horizontal artwork fills more wall space, horizontals outsell vertical pieces. Also, square pieces have become increasingly popular. Art consultants offer artists perspective that will increase their chances to sell more artwork to the corporate market.

Artists need art consultants and art consultants need artists. This mutually beneficial relationship is a strong bond, and since art consultants are not selling widgets, it becomes a very personally satisfying relationship. The consultant gives the artist feedback and art direction in an effort to place more artwork. The artist interprets the art direction and creates work in an attempt to meet the client's needs. Since artists are not present in meetings where their artwork is reviewed, they rely on consultants to give them feedback from decision makers.

Art consultants may give advice to artists about subject matter, color, composition, and present ideas that never occur to them. For example, in San Diego I often get requests for color photographs of recognizable landmarks and scenic beach landscapes. My clients do not like sunsets in the photographs, but my artists show me photographs with sunsets. Unless I clue my artists in, they will continue to take photographs with sunsets that will not be selected for my projects.

Another piece of advice I give artists is not to date their artwork when they sign it. I request a signature and title written on the artwork. If the piece is dated and does not sell within a reasonable amount of time, it is a disadvantage having the date appear on the artwork. When I explained this to several artists, they dropped the dates and thanked me for the feedback. It had never occurred to them that dating a piece could have an effect on selling it. I also advise my artists to have their name ghosted on each visual emailed for the purpose of showing images to potential clients. Why risk having the piece printed or copied by an unscrupulous person?

Before an artist makes an effort to find and work with an art consultant, he/she needs to be prepared and professional. Along with a professional portfolio of work, the artist needs to have an artist statement prepared as well as biographical information. The artist statement should be at least one page long and express the creative vision, methods, and style of the artwork produced. Artists tend to write about what inspires their personal style and particular influences that have directed them in the course of creating a body of work. If the artist has a certain method of producing their artwork, the statement should cite the process of achieving the work. Techniques should be discussed so that the reader can understand the artistic process. The biographical information should list juried and non-juried shows, education, published articles, and other pertinent data. Artists should update their statements and biographical information at least every two years.

Artists may find art consultants by contacting art galleries and art and framing companies. Since some independent art consultants work out of their homes, it may take some research for artists to find out who in their area is working on projects requiring art consultation. Artists may visit healthcare facilities, banks, hotels, and corporate spaces and ask who was responsible for the art program. By visiting spaces with good quality art and finding out who the art consultant was, artists can begin to determine who may be a good match in an artist/art consultant relationship. It is very educational to observe art programs, and by studying the artwork selected, it helps clarify solutions. Prolific artists should consider working with several art consultants at one time. Naturally it is easier to find a consultant in the same city, but expanding out of state will give artists more opportunity to move product. Different parts of the country have diverse economic climates. For example, it may be slow in California and steady in Texas. If an artist is serious about making a living selling artwork, having a business relationship with more than one consultant is prudent.

Another excellent way to find art consultants is through LinkedIn. Artists should strongly consider joining one of the art-related groups on LinkedIn such as one called Creative Art Consultants. Artists who join have access to the members who are both artists and art consultants. With a small investment of time, one can connect with art consultants in other parts of the country opening up doors to new business. Artists need to keep in mind that consultants are always looking for new artists, but they are busy people. Timing comes into play. Artists need to be patient and understand that just because an art consultant has not responded immediately to their inquiry does not mean there is no interest. Projects with deadlines take priority, and it may take some time and persistence for artists to connect with art consultants.

Art commissions

Some art consultants will act as a liaison between the artist and the decision maker when commissions are part of the art program. Many factors come into play when matching a suitable artist to a project. Customarily, following an extensive research phase including reviewing submissions from a variety of artists, the design committee will narrow down the candidates to the top three most promising artists. The short listed candidates will be interviewed by the art advisory committee and have an opportunity to express their vision and solution to the project.

Art commissions require additional agreements outlining the details of the commission and what is expected of both parties. Once an artist has been selected for a commission, a contract is signed spelling out all of the job requirements such as what the piece will look like, the scale, the materials to be used to execute the design, time lines, payment schedules, insurance, and installation. The artist may be responsible for producing sketches and dimensional miniature models to show his/her vision. It may be prudent to involve an attorney when composing a commission agreement the first time you are overseeing a commission. There are copyright laws that may need to be addressed. Art consultants work with their artists to help them find projects that require commissioned work.

When considering an artist for a commission the following points need to be considered:
1. What prior work experience does the artist have?
2. Has the artist worked on large-scale projects before?
3. Who are the artist's references?
4. What do the references say about the artist's working habits?
5. What is the artist's personality like? Is he/she easy to get along with?
6. How well does the artist communicate?
7. Does the artist have the technical abilities to produce what is required?
8. Can the artist meet the budget requirements of the project?

The difference between art that is consigned and art that is on memo

When an art consultant is preparing for a presentation, he/she starts to brainstorm and visualize which artists may be the best fit for the project. Most likely, the consultant will need to contact artists and art publishing companies to send artwork suitable for the new project. Some pieces may be in stock, and other pieces will need to be shipped in for review. This process involves checking websites of art publishing companies as well as communicating with your core artists.

If pieces are sent to you from an art publishing company for a short duration, the art is sent on memo. Once you have met with your client, the unsold pieces are sent back to the company. Art on memo is for presentation purposes. Art on consignment is artwork left for a longer period of time with the intent of having the consultant show it regularly. Consigned artwork is usually left with a consultant or art-related business for 6 to 12 months.

When I make a presentation for a specific job such as a healthcare facility, I show a combination of artwork on memo and consignment, along with my artist binders. My core artists work with me to send artwork on an as needed basis. Relationships I have with representatives from art publishing companies also prove to be invaluable in assisting me with getting artwork to show for presentations. Take the time to attend art-related trade shows and start a relationship with art publishing companies. The West Coast Art and Frame Show held annually is a wonderful venue to make these contacts.

Art publishers and Art dealers

In addition to working with your own artists, art publishers and art dealers offer more sources to show your prospective clients. Art publishers understand the corporate art market and have the financial backing to produce innovative artwork printed on surfaces such as canvas, acrylic, metal, and plyboo (a sustainable bamboo plywood). Having catalogs from art publishers and browsing their websites periodically will increase your chances of finding supplemental pieces to show your clients. Understandably, it is difficult to predict which pieces a decision maker will select, therefore it is best to have access to artwork from publishers and dealers to the trade. After considering your own artists for a project, fill in with artwork from these alternate sources. Be sure to have updated catalogs from several art publishing companies, especially ones that cater to the corporate buyer. Some art publishers will ship artwork on memo by special request. Each company works differently, but it is worth investigating art publishers, because they do have some excellent corporate art at fair prices.

Art publishers introduce new artists and release new works regularly. Open editions and large editions keep prices quite competitive. With the advent of giclee printing, art publishers no longer have the expense of printing an entire edition at once. Pieces are printed on demand (POD) and inventories are kept low to reduce expenses. Another advantage in working with art publishers is the flexibility of offering giclees in several different standard sizes. Custom sizes are available as well. Art publishers have inventory available to send upon request. With the size flexibility and price factor, art consultants should always check art publishing companies when pulling together artwork for a presentation.

Art dealers, also referred to as art brokers, work as a liaison between the artist and the art consultant. Whereas, art publishing companies sell to all design professionals, art dealers decide to whom they want to sell. Art dealers help their artists develop portfolios of artwork, and many of these artists are available for commissions. Generally, an art consultant will communicate with an art dealer regarding a project and then set up an appointment to review the pieces available that fit the color palette, size, budget, and subject matter. Pieces of interest are left on memo to the art consultant for presentation purposes. If a meeting cannot be arranged between the art dealer and the art consultant due to logistics, artwork may be shipped either in a flat package or rolled in a tube. I have worked with several art dealers over the years, and on many occasions their artists were a perfect fit for the project. Think of art dealers as professional partners to assist you with problem solving and increasing your art offerings. Since art dealers work diligently to find new artists, each time you meet with them there is something new and fresh to see.

The lesson here is to be open to suggestions and try showing a variety of artwork. On occasion, an art consultant will get an unusual request for a specific kind of artwork. For example, I had a client requesting black and white photographic images of simple architectural features from modern buildings. The images needed to be outdoor facades of unrecognizable buildings. Unable to locate the right images from my core group of artists, one of my art dealers was able to find exactly what my client envisioned. Overall, art dealers have a keen sense in finding artists, and art consultants that are prudent in business use their services.

Why consider using art publishing companies and art dealers?
1. Access to more artists
2. Artwork printed on a variety of substrates such as acrylic, metal, and wood
3. Good value, especially open editions and large editions
4. Print on Demand (POD) offers a variety of sizes available
5. Assistance with problem solving for unusual requests by clients
6. Minimal cost to have a larger selection of images for presentations
7. Catalogs from art publishers are excellent selling tools

Summary of working with artists

Working with artists can be challenging, so keep all these tips in mind to have successful relationships. Treat your artists with respect, pay them on time, communicate regularly, and keep them abreast of your projects. Maintain good records and request new work from them to keep the inventory fresh. Having a large stable of wonderful artists will help you succeed in closing many corporate jobs. Make an effort to add new artists to your core group. After all, this is one way you can control how you set yourself apart from your competition.

Chapter 13

Healthcare Facilities

The field of healthcare offers a variety of ongoing opportunities for art consultants. In both challenging and healthy economic climates, the healthcare sector remains a steady and buoyant market due to population growth, population aging, and the need to update older facilities with new technology. Increasingly, since the millennium, medical facilities including hospitals, clinics, senior living residences, and dental and medical offices have recognized the importance of providing healing and aesthetically pleasing environments. Art budgets are factored in when preliminary budgets for furniture, lighting, signage, floor and wall treatments, and other essential furnishings are presented to project managers during the early stages of construction. Artwork is no longer looked at as frivolous; it is an integral part of the design plan.

Public artwork serves many functions in healthcare facilities. Strategically placed artwork helps soothe and welcome patients and visitors. It also assists with wayfinding. Artwork helps clarify the boundaries of public and non-public areas of hospitals. Common areas displaying artwork are entrances, waiting rooms, corridors, patient rooms, and cafeterias. Usually, art consultants working on healthcare projects are part of a design team, and a committee of decision makers such as the project manager, architect, interior designer, facilities manager, and administrators makes art selections.

In hospitals, the goals of the design team are to incorporate the benefits of environmental sustainability while designing an uplifting environment conducive to healing. The artwork selected is theme based, with the most common theme being nature and its beauty. From poster art to high-end sculptures, nature themed artwork is specified and purchased in new and remodeled healthcare facilities. While neighborhood clinics and doctors' offices may require a substantial amount of artwork, hospitals require art programs much larger in scale. The artwork specified in new hospitals complements cutting-edge architectural design and adds to the ambiance of the space. With such features as atriums, waterfalls, etched and stained glass walls, and large open spaces with natural lighting, the demand for upscale artwork is high. Artwork is part of the equation to introduce a harmonious and uplifting environment for patients. It is equally important to the staff working at the facility.

Healthcare administrators and their committees are open to purchasing a variety of types of artwork from photographs, one-of-a-kind mixed media pieces, paintings on canvas, ceramic and metal wall pieces, to all kind of sculptures. Reproductions such as posters are often used in patient rooms. Color palettes are inspired by nature ranging from soft to deeper greens, as well as beige, brown, yellow, amber, and blue. With sensitivity to blood, the color red is generally avoided or used only slightly as an accent color.

The trend in healthcare is green and sustainable design. In this era of environmental concern, it is compulsory that architects and designers adapt to integrating new systems that affect external and internal factors such as energy efficiency, water use, and indoor air quality. LEED, the Leadership in Energy and Environmental Design, plays a significant role in directing green design of new and future medical facilities with incentives and ratings awarded for sustainability and environmental protection.

The type of artwork specified for a particular kind of facility varies depending on the population being served. Senior residences usually have artwork that is more traditional than artwork installed in a typical medical office. While newer hospitals may use some abstract work mixed with contemporary nature motifs, senior assisted living communities tend to specify landscapes with gardens and florals, and generally do not opt for abstract images. Regions of the country also have defined looks, such as tropical and beach in California and Florida versus scenes of full foliage and pastures in the Midwest.

Although challenging, entering the healthcare market can provide a new revenue stream. To test the market and build up confidence, start by bidding on smaller medical and dental offices. It is a gradual process to work up to higher budget jobs. In order to be considered for larger jobs, years of experience are essential. Understandably, decision makers at a new or remodeled hospital will not turn over an art program to an art consultant who has not demonstrated expertise and past performance.

It has been my experience in southern California that hospitals require art consultants and art installers to take dust maintenance classes, contractor protocol classes, and to pass a double set of TB tests. Consultants do not need badges to make a proposal, but if they are intending to participate in the art installations, badges are necessary. Badges with photo identification are issued to art consultants and their installers once they have completed the necessary paperwork including proof of immunizations. Badges are issued annually and art consultants cannot work in a hospital without wearing a current badge. It is the responsibility of the consultant to be on top of getting badges renewed. If consultants and their installers do not follow contractor protocol, such as dust and debris cleanup, they may be asked to leave the hospital. This can, of course, seriously impact your chances of being rehired for future projects.

At all times, art consultants need to be sensitive to the hospital environment and notify staff about noise expectations during the installation. If it is necessary to ask a patient or visitor to move while installing in waiting rooms, the installation crew should always be polite. When installers are loading carts of artwork and equipment into elevators, they should always give medical staff and visitors the courtesy of using the elevator first.

In some hospitals, art consultants and their installers are escorted to the security office before unloading the artwork. At times, art consultants and their installers may be fingerprinted. Some hospitals require a staff member to be with the installers at all times. Areas such as the Intensive Care Unit or Burn Unit may take extra time for installation due to the condition of the patients. Unexpected circumstances such as infectious diseases in the ICU may prohibit installers from entering rooms, which means return trips need to be scheduled. Understanding the hospital's procedures is important. Because there are protocols that must be followed, art consultants cannot schedule an installation a day or two before the art needs to be hung; it has to be planned and scheduled at least 2 - 3 weeks in advance. With unforeseen circumstances, healthcare installations may require return trips and extra time. Keep this in mind when trying to estimate how long an installation will take.

When completing an installation at a healthcare facility or any corporate job, our company presents a receiving form that is signed by the project manager. The form lists the number of pieces installed, the purchase order, the address of the job site, the contact person, and the date. It is critical to have a signed delivery receipt, especially when trying to get paid for a job. In several cases when tracking overdue receivables, I have been asked to send proof that all of the artwork was received. Make a point of getting a signed delivery receipt for all finished work.

Getting on board with healthcare companies can be a time consuming and tedious process. Pages of forms must be submitted with information about workers compensation, insurance, business documents, banking, references, etc. Contracts are lengthy. Turnaround times are sometimes unrealistic. With that being said, working in the field of healthcare can be satisfying and lucrative. It takes a very detailed, focused, and hard working individual to succeed.

Types of healthcare facilities:
1. Hospitals
2. Clinics
3. Outpatient facilities
4. Senior living residences and assisted living facilities
5. Dental offices
6. Medical offices
7. Occupational therapy and rehabilitation centers
8. Cancer and medical research centers
9. Eye clinics

Art consultants working with hospital staff may also be called upon to coordinate the framing of donor portraits, promotional ads, historical photographs, awards and certificates, and display cases containing memorabilia and historical items belonging to the hospital. One hospital we worked with had us reframe 150 donor portraits dating back over 50 years. Each portrait had to be identified and a brass plate made with the donor's name. Some photographs needed restoration. The original identification plates were missing on some photographs and, consequently, we had to work with the hospital archives department to research and make proper identifications. Another job in a psychiatric area of a hospital required us to round the corners of the joined wood frames so there were no sharp corners for possible self inflicted injury. Medical facilities not only need artwork, but they need an art consultant who knows framing design well enough to solve the many situations that may arise.

Goals of healthcare artwork and framing:
1. To soothe and welcome patients, visitors, and staff.
2. To assist with wayfinding.
3. To reduce stress and create a healing environment.
4. To add visual interest and complement architectural features.
5. To display and archive historical information.
6. To display mission statements and information pertinent to client safety.
7. To display ads and promotional material.

Guidelines for selecting healthcare artwork:

1. Nature related subject matter.
2. Soothing color palette, with little or no red.
3. Avoid threatening subject matter such as scenery with cliffs.
4. Peaceful landscapes such as meadows, gardens, and fields of flowers.
5. Images depicting summer, fall, and spring.
6. Avoid images that can be interpreted as lonely and deserted scenes such as empty piers on a beach.
7. No photographs of people with recognizable faces.
8. Steer away from abstract artwork in patient rooms, especially in psychiatric patient rooms.
9. Avoid scenes with sharp objects such as rugged rocks or jagged trees.

Some hospitals or clinics require an artist identification plate hung next to the artwork. The identification usually lists the artist's name, title of the piece, date the piece was created, and what type of medium (such as giclee, photograph, mixed media, etc). In a neighborhood healthcare clinic requesting artist identification information, our company prepared the computer graphics and fabricated acrylic covers with sanded edges. The covers were attached to the wall using brass escutcheon pins inserted through predrilled holes in the acrylic. When making identification plates, be sure to charge appropriately and to confirm with the client that the cards are formatted to their standards. It is a good idea to have a proof of the output approved by a responsible party.

Healthcare clients offer an ongoing opportunity for art consultants to have a steady flow of work as a result of upgrading facilities, remodeling efforts, and through expansions of additional buildings. Often one department receiving artwork will spur an interest in other departments requesting artwork. Some art consultants with a good grip on providing solutions will specialize in healthcare art and not work with other types of clients. The projects are large scale in comparison to selling 10 to 20 pieces for a corporate office. It is definitely a market worth exploring.

The power of artwork cannot be underestimated. I began my career as an art therapist working with sexually abused girls in a residential treatment center. Art creating sessions provided a point of departure for the girls to discuss family issues. During one art therapy session, a girl actually drew a picture of the person who had molested her. Up until that point, she could not verbally express the trauma. The drawing was used as evidence in court to convict her stepfather, the man who had molested her. I testified in court with the drawing. From that point on in my career, I understood the power of artwork as a form of self expression.

Artwork in healthcare facilities evokes emotion. Connecting with nature is in our DNA and viewing nature related artwork instills a sense of calm within us. Interior designers discuss evidenced based design and have been conducting studies with the purpose of showing a documented relationship between the use of nature related artwork and its healing properties. Evidenced based design will become a familiar phrase that will be part of the dialogue when art consultants and design professionals specify artwork in the years to come.

Chapter 14

Hospitality Clients

Hotels, resorts, and restaurants open a wide range of possibilities for public artwork. In a hotel or resort setting, artwork is specified in corridors, reception areas, restaurants, spas, workout rooms, ballrooms, conference rooms, and individual rooms. In addition, some facilities have separate timeshare buildings and golf centers. There is a vast amount of artwork possibilities at many different price points. While smaller boutique hotels may opt for poster art and some fine art in their lobby, upscale hotels often have substantial art budgets purchasing large canvases, sculptures, wall hangings, and mixed media pieces. The artwork is directly tied to the ambiance and scale of luxury in the hotel.

Finding the decision makers in hospitality projects may be challenging, as many developers reside out of town. Large design firms often have contracts to supply all of the furnishings including artwork and framed mirrors. If you are able to identify which design firms have contracts with the hotels you are researching, it may be possible to get on board. The more services you can offer, the better chances you will have to be considered for a project. For example, our firm has been hired numerous times to fabricate and install mirrors for hotel rooms. Once we had a connection, it opened the door to many art and framing opportunities. Maintenance of existing artwork, such as replacing broken glass and damaged frames is another service to offer.

Subscribing to Hospitality Design Magazine, is a good starting point to learn about current styles and trends. The magazine also publishes a resource directory listing design firms and contact information. The key is to do your homework and be prepared with a variety of artwork should you decide to enter this market.

In proposing hotel room art, is imperative to understand digital printing. Art consultants may be required to design and print digital output on paper and canvas for room art. Some consultants invest in their own large format printers to keep costs down. Security installations are the norm, and due to the scale of projects, scaffolds are needed to reach high walls. In remodeled hotels, the artwork may be specified in phases to keep the occupancy at certain levels. In all cases, when preparing a proposal, specify that the facility needs to be ready to receive the artwork on the date of delivery. Put a clause in the proposal stating that return trips will incur additional charges. Also, be sure to get a deposit, as hospitality clients are notorious for being slow paying. Inevitably there are construction delays.

Hospitality artwork has a unique feel quite different from artwork specified for healthcare or office environments. Visit new hotels in your area to achieve an understanding of the types, scale, and variety of artwork displayed. Often, the artwork is theme oriented or specific to a geographic area. This is a market that takes time, dedication, and experience to be successful. Should you be interested in pursuing hospitality projects, start with smaller hotels and work up to medium and larger scale projects. The good news is that if you work with hotels having multiple locations, the work will keep coming your way.

Types of hospitality clients:
Hotels
Spas
Restaurants
Health Clubs
Golf Clubs
Country Clubs
Timeshares
Casinos
Nightclubs and Bars
Convention Centers
Racetracks

Chapter 15

Branding, Marketing, and Creating a Community Presence

All business owners want to stand out from their competition and present viable ways to promote their businesses to potential clients. A seasoned art consultant may have a definite advantage over a newcomer to the profession. Regardless of how long you have been in business, having a marketing plan to increase your client base is essential. Whether you hire an outside agency or create your own marketing plan, take the time and energy to figure out a strategy and implement it. Change it as your business evolves. Mix it up so it is not stagnant. Vary your ads depending on the target market you are going after.

In an industry where creativity and design interplays with practical business, it is often hard to focus on what aspect of your company to market. I have found a combination of methods work for me. The important aspects of my business that I continually try to promote are the length of time I have been in business, my extensive client list, the artists I represent, the full services I offer including in-house picture framing and installation services, and my national recognition as a writer and lecturer for the art and picture framing industry. Whatever your strengths, offerings, and unique qualities are, market them.

Since I enjoy writing and I understand my business better than an outside party, many of my business promotions involve writing about my company. Writing and speaking about your business opens a variety of avenues to solicit business that are free and will keep your name in the public's eye. We all know the power of the written word, and seizing the opportunity to write as well as speak about your business will set you apart from your competition. Whether it is a newsletter or meeting of the local chapter of American Society of Interior Designers (ASID) or your local business journal, step up and volunteer to write or speak about your business. This free exposure will go a long way in bringing you name recognition in your local community.

Try writing an educational article about some aspect of your business for a local publication. I have written articles for the San Diego ASID chapter newsletter on the subjects of framing and why people buy art. After attending a tabletop expo event with our local ASID chapter, I wrote an article on networking and submitted a photograph of myself from the event. Not only did I get the article published with an accompanying photograph, but the free publicity led to several jobs with interior designers who read the article. I also write articles for Picture Framing Magazine on the subjects of networking, art consultation, and business promotion. Writing for a national magazine sets me apart from my local competition and helps position me as an expert. The point is to look for local and national opportunities to write about some aspect of your business. The free publicity will help establish you as an expert and raise your visibility in the community. In addition, published articles will increase your search engine optimization. If a prospective client does an online search for "art consultant" and you have a published article on this subject, the chances are your name will appear before your competitor's name. Every bit of advantage and exposure helps.

Schools, religious organizations, and other nonprofit organizations regularly approach our company to donate items to fundraisers. Our policy is to always give a merchandise certificate. By donating a merchandise certificate, our company's name appears in the public eye year round in a variety of settings with different people attending. Many of the merchandise certificates are never redeemed, but our name is still associated with the fundraiser. Goodwill goes a long way in associating your company with charitable events. The investment is small in exchange for the rewards.

Partnering with nonprofit charitable organizations and offering either framing or artwork is another excellent way to gain exposure for your business. Not only is there an altruistic factor in giving back to your community, but also the publicity associated with the event attracts the types of people you want as clients. Our company partnered with a local bank (one of our clients) offering furnishings for a facility housing battered women and their children. We designed and framed all of the artwork for the facility. The publicity was very positive and several local newspapers mentioned our company. Every year our company donates framing for the local Alzheimer's Association that brings us unframed artwork done by patients. The pieces are framed and auctioned off at an annual fundraiser event. These types of donations show your business is supportive and caring to local issues and concerns. Giving back to your community is a "feel good" way to keep your name in the spotlight.

Speaking about your business can be as simple as offering to be a guest lecturer in a college course on gallery management or design. Offer to be on a panel at an ASID meeting or take it even further by speaking at events held in art related businesses. Art consultants can host Continuing Education Units (CEU) classes at their businesses and speak about art and framing design. Look for opportunities to speak about your business.

There are endless opportunities to gain exposure by speaking and writing about your business or partnering with a community organization. A balance of relatively inexpensive strategies may be blended with a first-rate website and some advertising. Hiring a website designer can be expensive, but the pay off will be worth it. A well designed website will give your company a site to showcase artists and photographs of finished installations. An interactive website will indeed put you on a more level playing field with your competitors. Blogs will also help you gain exposure. Since our company offers custom picture framing in addition to corporate art consultation services, many of the ideas I have presented may be too broad for your situation. Clearly branding and marketing will increase your client base, strengthen your uniqueness, and differentiate you from your competition. To capture a larger cross section of the marketplace, reshape your branding, try new methods, and study approaches by your competitors.

Marketing and branding tips:
1. Take advantage of free exposure such as writing and speaking about your business.
2. Give out merchandise certificates to gain exposure year round.
3. Form an alliance with a nonprofit organization and donate your services.

4. Have an interactive website showcasing your artists and projects.
5. Write a blog.
6. Utilize social networking sites such as LinkedIn, Twitter, and Facebook.
7. Vary your copy depending on the target audience.
8. Market your strengths and uniqueness to set yourself apart from your competition.
9. Study what your competitors are doing.
10. Reshape and evaluate regularly.

Chapter 16

Working With Interior Designers

Interior designers rely on art and framing companies to provide endless sources of artwork and framing for their projects. While interior designers may actually specify the art program for a particular project, when it comes to artwork their resources are much more limited than those of an art consultant or art and framing company. Understandably, since art consultants expend a tremendous amount of effort in regularly adding new artists, they are able to offer more options to the end user. Specifying artwork is only one service that an interior designer may offer, whereas the primary focus of art consultants is to develop and implement art programs. Art consultants work with interior designers and space planers in several different ways.

A common way for interior designers and art consultants to work together is as team members on projects. The interior designer charges their client an hourly fee for this service. The art consultant assists in problem solving by suggesting artists that will work for the project. Usually a discount is extended to the client, and the bookkeeping goes through the art consultant's business. The role of the art consultant in this scenario is to meet with the interior designer, select the artwork, submit a proposal, complete the order, and coordinate the installation. The interior designer brings to the meeting either blueprints or a floor plan along with fabric samples, furniture finishes, paint colors, and flooring samples. By looking at the traffic flow of the environment and discussing primary areas, both the interior designer and art consultant determine the number of pieces, size of the artwork, and the art placement.

In some cases, the art consultant will be asked to bring the artwork and frame samples to the client for approval. More often than not, the client trusts the interior designer to select appropriate artwork within a certain budget range. Visuals of the images are emailed as part of the proposal. When it comes time for installation, both the art consultant and the interior designer work together to finalize art placement. Art consultants have many ongoing relationships with interior designers that work in this fashion, and repeat business usually occurs as one job is completed and another one is in the pipeline. The interior designer partners with the art consultant in an effort to give their client the highest level of professional art services.

Another way interior designers work with art consultants is to bring their clients to the art showroom for a scheduled meeting. This way of conducting business is contingent on whether or not the art consultant has a business location outside of their home. If a showroom or gallery space is available to show artwork and framing design, working this way can be very beneficial. Most likely, if the art consultant works out of their home, this type of arrangement would probably not be an option.

Communication before the scheduled meeting should center on the terms of the transaction. Some interior designers forego their interior designer discounts and instead pass along the discount to their retail clients. Some interior designers come with their corporate clients to select actual pieces for projects and ask that the pieces selected be brought to the client's place of business. The key is to understand before the meeting what the interior designer hopes to accomplish and what the terms of the sale will be. When in doubt, always quote retail pricing when an interior designer comes to you with a client. After the meeting, the details can be worked out to clarify any gray areas.

Interior designers may meet with an art consultant at the showroom with the intention of selecting unframed artwork to show their client. In this situation, the art consultant is less involved in the art program. Suggestions are made with the goal of choosing artwork that will be memoed out for a short period of time. All artwork selected will be recorded on a memo agreement which clearly states the duration of the agreement, value, and condition of the artwork. Routinely, unsold pieces are returned, and each piece is reviewed to check for any damages. Returned artwork cannot simply be dropped off in a stack at a design counter. Both parties must take the time to check in each piece against the memo agreement. Some art consultants take a credit card number as a security measure until the artwork is returned safely. The other point to consider is whether or not the pieces on memo will be needed to show in-house clients for projects. Most importantly, an art consultant should not temporarily deplete their inventory to the extent that when meeting with their own clients they cannot present a strong art selection.

Working with interior designers can be lucrative, especially when it involves repeat business. In some circumstances, an interior designer will be part of a design team with the art consultant, architect, project manager, and other team members. Here the interior designer's role is to specify the furniture, lighting, wall treatment, flooring, and coordinate ordering. While the art consultant will drive the art selection process, the interior designer and other team members will have some input. This happens quite often on larger projects where art is specified on many floors of an office building or in a healthcare facility.

In recent years, with the availability of purchasing artwork from artists directly or through art publishers, some interior designers have taken on the role of art adviser. On smaller jobs, the outcome may be successful, but on large jobs where a variety of artwork is required, the interior designer may not have a full range of art offerings. Additionally, another problem is that all of the solutions begin to look the same due to the limited amount of resources. The profession of interior design is to be respected, but when it comes to artwork, an art consultant should be respected as well. The end user deserves to have the best options available. While interior designers are fully capable of specifying framed art posters, when it comes to fine art specified for a large project, I believe an art consultant should be brought into the equation.

Framing is usually a key component of the art program, and since interior designers do not offer in-house picture framing, they turn to art consultants or picture framers to assist in this area. Art consultants are up to speed on current picture framing materials and trends. Framing is complex, and with an infinite amount of options, can be very time consuming to design. Each individual component of the design needs to be priced out to determine a final price. For example, posters need to be mounted, but fine art does not. Mixed media pieces on paper may need a spacer, while some flat art does not. Canvas pieces need stretching and stretcher bars, but paper art does not. Interior designers work with art consultants to create innovative and distinctive picture framing that is also cost effective.

Art consultants and interior designers have many different methods of working together. Mutual respect for their areas of expertise is necessary for a smooth and professional working relationship. Art consultants should strongly consider joining their local chapter of the American Society of Interior Designers (ASID). Meetings are informative and offer excellent networking opportunities.

Chapter 17

Meeting Deadlines

Without a doubt, if there is one highly valuable skill necessary to succeed as an art consultant, it would be the ability to follow through in a timely manner. Each signed contract will have phases of the project that need special attention in order to meet deadlines. While you may be juggling several jobs simultaneously, art and framing materials need to be ordered, installations scheduled, work orders written to specify framing designs, tubes of artwork opened and inspected, and new proposals sent out.

Organization is the key to servicing all accounts in a way that makes your client feel you are meeting or better yet surpassing their expectations. Review each active account daily to address how the job is proceeding. Communicate with your clients and let them know how their job is progressing. Do not wait until the day before the installation to touch base with your clients.

It goes without saying that in the corporate world, deadlines are part of the game. Clearly, if you want to be a serious player, make a personal commitment to meet deadlines. This means getting proposals out on time, making presentations on time, and overseeing all projects on time. Installation dates cannot be rescheduled easily, especially when they are scheduled around furniture and plant deliveries. Choose your vendors carefully, and make sure they can deliver. You may subcontract all of your framing or certain aspects of a large job such as volume mounting or cutting acrylic with the understanding that deadlines are mandatory. As a precaution, build in a few extra days of cushion when promising large volume jobs.

Again, this is another way to plow ahead of your competition. Unquestionably, do what you say you will do, keep your word, and follow through on time. Your reputation as a reliable and trustworthy businessperson is extremely important. You may believe all corporate art consultants are sensitive to deadlines; I have found the contrary. Business executives want to maintain relationships with consultants who deliver on time, communicate effectively, provide value, and follow through on their proposals.

Chapter 18

Setting Yourself Apart From Your Competition

Realistically, you will not win all of the accounts you hope to. Some accounts you would like to have are already "happily" working with a competing art consultant. This is a reality. Why does your competitor have an account that you do not? Your competitor has a solid relationship based on trust, value, and service. Sometimes, you can manage to get an appointment with the decision maker and sway the business your way. Other times you will hit a wall.

Knowing what your competitors are doing and how you can offer more will open up opportunities to win new business. For example, I have won over accounts that have had relationships with my competitors when it became apparent I could offer in-house custom framing and my competitor could not. My prices were comparable, but my turnaround times were quicker and selection of frames larger, therefore the decision maker switched over to using my services. The lesson here is to differentiate yourself from your competition and go after accounts even when they are already using another art consultant. Naturally, you will not get every account, but with the mindset of setting yourself apart from your competition and with emphasis on persistence, you will increase your business opportunities.

Also know what your competitors are doing. Look at their websites and ads, and visit their installed jobs. It is a combination of the following strategies that will give you a competitive edge:

1. Network and join at least one group with exclusivity in the category of art consultant.
2. Regularly add new artists.
3. Meet all deadlines.
4. Use telemarketing.
5. Follow up on leads from your tickler file.
6. Acknowledge all referrals you receive.
7. Send handwritten thank you notes.
8. Form alliances with business networking friends.
9. Schedule Lunch and Learns.
10. Write and speak about your business.
11. Attend clients' opening parties and holiday events.
12. Invite your best clients to networking functions.
13. Show innovative framing design.
14. Make new business contacts each month.
15. Identify your competitors' weaknesses and use this information to your advantage.
16. Communicate with your clients regularly.
17. Show inspiring and technically appropriate framing design. Step up the framing design

and use high-grade materials.

18. Call on referrals immediately.
19. Utilize the benefits of social networking.
20. Market your strengths and uniqueness.
21. Build client relationships by keeping track of clients' interests and family information.
22. Use a framing company with at least one Certified Picture Framer on staff.
23. Ask for testimonial letters from all satisfied clients.
24. Work with many local artists who create local recognizable scenes.
25. Change your marketing strategy regularly.

Chapter 19

Training Employees to Become Art Consultants

I teach in my classes that business owners should take the initiative to lead their company in corporate art sales. Employees come and go, but as a business owner you are a constant who can nurture, cultivate, and maintain important business relationships. When training employees to become art consultants, proceed with caution, especially when your goal is to turn over accounts. From experience, I understand the upside to having a motivated sales person on staff who can close corporate sales. I also know the downside that happens when a former employee becomes an independent art consultant calling on company clients. Since your former employee took the initiative to create strong, productive relationships, client loyalty does not always work in your favor. The person you trained knows your methods, pricing, artists, and more. For this reason, I say proceed with caution when training staff to become art consultants.

This is not to say do not train your employees to assist with the corporate art division of your company. In recent years, I have had many assistants helping me with presentations and proposals. However, I am at the helm, taking full responsibility for all of the art consultation projects coming through my business. Decision makers have a relationship with me, and I take care of my clients. Having employees who understand the process helps, especially with administrative duties. Should you decide to train your employees to go after corporate art sales, keep the communication open. Schedule weekly sales meetings to discuss strategies, and touch base regarding the status of all projects. If you have multiple sales staff, determine how to distribute leads and accounts. It can be done geographically dividing territories within the city. The method you use to divide up accounts needs to be equitable. Openly discussing what each of your employees is doing will help alleviate problems in overlapping accounts. Situations will come up at weekly meetings. It is important to address solutions in an effort to keep everyone working as a team and diffuse ill feelings that can paralyze a work force.

Know what your employees are doing, and review all written communication before it is sent out. Remember employees are representing your company and its image. Check for pricing errors in proposals; it is important to catch them before the proposals are sent out. If written communication contains poor grammar, it needs to be corrected. As a training measure, distribute sample proposals and business letters so employees can obtain an idea of company standards. If your policy is for all employees to write a personal thank you note following completion of projects, make sure the procedure is being followed.

When hiring or training an employee, confirm they will conform to the company's dress code. Having art consultants on staff is a time consuming process, because you need to schedule regular meetings and completely understand performance levels. Be forthright with expectations regarding company procedures. Invest the necessary time to monitor actions, otherwise your business and reputation may suffer.

In the 1990s, our company employed several corporate art sales representatives, and the combined leadership talent was strong. Regular meetings addressed strategies and job updates. Policies were put in place and protocols followed. For example, our company policy stated commissions would be paid only on orders that were free of mistakes. In sending jobs through to our frame shop, many things could have gone wrong such as errors in measuring, incorrect framing materials specified, not charging for all of the framing methods required, and extending unauthorized discounts. Mistakes are costly; determine your own company policies on how to handle situations with errors.

Be sure to have policies in writing defining the roles of employee and supervisor. When an employee is on a sales call, have a sign-out sheet informing you whom the meeting is with, the address, company phone number, and the purpose of the meeting. This is particularly important in case you need to reach your employee. Know where your sales representatives are at all times.

Involve your sales staff in getting deposits and balances due for their projects. It was our company policy to withhold paying commissions until the clients paid in full. Sales representatives were held responsible for calling clients late on paying their invoices, and they were motivated to collect receivables knowing that it affected their paychecks. Our sales representatives understood monthly sales reports were taken seriously and were to be turned in on time. Late sales reports meant commissions were not paid until the following month. The point is to set and adhere to policies and have consequences if the policies are not followed.

How do you determine when an employee is producing enough sales to justify the position of corporate art consultant? Obviously, each business has different overhead expenses. Nonetheless, take into account that there is a learning curve, and do not expect immediate results. Your sales representative should be closing a significant amount of business. Sales will be slow the first six months, but after that sales should increase monthly as new clients are serviced. You may need to do some number crunching with your accountant to understand what monthly figures need to be achieved in order to be profitable.

In an effort to protect proprietary information, it is advisable to draft a noncompetition agreement between the business owner and sales representative. Consult an attorney to draft an agreement outlining the parameters of the relationship. Although you may fully trust your employees, relationships change over the course of time. Recognize and document the names of all pre-existing clients your employees bring to your business. In the hiring process discuss how you will handle compensation for business your new employee may bring to you from their own client base. The noncompetition agreement should state that employees may neither use proprietary information nor contact clients or artists within one year following their departure from the company. Exceptions to the agreement would be pre-existing clients that employees bring to the company at the time of employment. Keep a signed copy of the agreement in the employee's file and mention it will be enforced. Although in reality the agreement may not stop all former employees from contacting company clients or using company material, hopefully it will discourage them and instill a moral obligation within them to respect proprietary information. Unfortunately, business people are free to choose whom to work with and may opt to continue working with your former employee, who is now one of your competitors.

Having a team of art consultants on staff is a large commitment. The following are tips to consider when writing and implementing procedures for your sales team:

1. Have all company policies in writing. Distribute copies that are read and signed by all staff. Retain a copy in each employee's file.
2. Schedule weekly sales meetings to discuss leads, projects, and strategies.
3. Determine how to distribute leads and accounts.
4. Read all written correspondence and proposals before being sent out.
5. Do not pay commissions on projects where errors cost the company money.
6. Do not pay commissions until the client has paid in full.
7. Have a sign-out sheet to be filled out for all outside appointments.
8. Use your authority to remove a sales representative from an account for violating company policy or not servicing the account to company standards.
9. Draft a noncompetition agreement to help protect against former employees from contacting clients or using proprietary information.

Chapter 20

Packaging, Shipping, and Receiving Artwork

Sending and receiving artwork is routine for art consultants. Rolled artwork arrives in tubes and should be inspected before signing for the goods. Tubes that are damaged should not be accepted unless the condition is noted at the time of receipt. When dealing with art publishing companies, it may be prudent to reject all damaged tubes, call the vendor to report the damages, and request a replacement tube to be sent out immediately. Filing claims is a time-consuming process, therefore refusing the shipment tends to be a better solution. This is of course only applicable to artwork that is replaceable such as posters, giclees, and photographs. Customarily, when shipping artwork, it is insured for its replacement value. Art consultants need to take full responsibility for insuring and properly packaging artwork that needs to be returned to artists or publishing companies.

Artwork received should be opened within 5 working days and inspected for printing flaws, creases, scratches, tears, or any other damages. Report all damages immediately and resolve the situation. When receiving artwork from poster companies, review the accompanying packing list to confirm what you received matches what was ordered. It is fairly common to receive incorrect posters, especially with large orders. In addition, the packing list will note posters out of stock or no longer available. Unfortunately, when ordering posters for clients, art consultants are not always able to fulfill the order 100% due to limited availability of some images. As a precaution, it is wise to specify a few alternate posters, which can be substituted in case the posters you need are unavailable.

Since artwork removed from a tube is quite curly, flatten it out by putting weights on each corner. Flat artwork is much easier to work with, especially when trying to measure and design it for framing. Weights can be purchased at an art supply store. The weights our company uses are a soft leather that will not scratch or harm the artwork.

When rolling artwork to ship back to artists, art brokers, or art publishers, take special care to package the artwork correctly. Roll the artwork in brown paper allowing approximately 2 - 3 inches of space at both ends of the tube. Place bubble wrap or tissue paper inside each end of the tube to serve as a buffer. Roll the artwork slightly smaller than the circumference of the tube. When wound too tightly, the artwork will move around during shipping, possibly causing damage. Pay special attention to how poster companies ship their posters and learn from their methods. Keep the tubes you receive and reuse them.

Shipping flat artwork requires more structural packaging material to ensure that it does not bend. Artwork is sandwiched between two pieces of plywood or a similar material. Corrugated cardboard may be used on one side to reduce the weight of the package. However, two pieces of corrugated cardboard taped together with the parallel lines going in the same direction is not a good idea, because the package will be prone to bending. If you alternate the orientation of the corrugated cardboard, it works better, but when in doubt, over package rather than under package.

Art consultants regularly administrate shipping and crating of artwork for their clients. If your company cannot build crates, find a reliable source that will be able to fabricate custom crates for artwork. In servicing national and regional accounts, the ability to oversee crating of artwork is a necessity. Building custom crates for artwork is not inexpensive and needs to be factored in as a cost of doing business. Also, the added time to build crates should be considered when meeting deadlines.

Keeping track of artwork for jobs can be challenging, especially when tubes arrive containing artwork for multiple jobs. Checking in artwork can be tedious and time consuming. Art consultants regularly ship and receive artwork and need to ensure the proper care of artwork at all times. Procedures and forms will help document the process. For example, our company has a receiving form filled out daily, logging in all shipments. Another form called a damage and discrepancy form is filled out to document merchandise arriving damaged or not what was ordered. Since our company protocol is not to approve payment of damaged or incorrect goods, this form is invaluable. Create your own procedures and forms to document the flow of artwork through your company. Taking the extra time to implement procedures will help alleviate many problems in this area.

Chapter 21

Testimonials and Letters of Recommendation

No doubt an impressive client list is advantageous to show to prospective clients, but better yet are testimonials and letters of recommendation. One of the problems with a client list is that it does not indicate how much business was actually done. An art consultant may have only framed two posters for a client and added them to their client list. Another competing art consultant may have completed a large job for the same company. The same client appears on both of their lists. However, a letter of recommendation or a testimonial from a client will be far more informative and may assist in closing sales.

Having a respectable, high profile executive vouch for your problem solving abilities, customer service, extensive art selection, value, and craftsmanship will definitely ease some concerns new clients may have in bringing you on board as their art consultant. Previously, I discussed the importance of influential business people spreading the word about you through their networks. An equally important strategy is to present endorsement letters to skeptical decision makers who do not know you, but may likely know the people who endorse you. What other high profile business people say about you has power, giving you an edge over your competition. For example, if you have successfully completed several jobs in the healthcare sector and have testimonials from the decision makers, showing these endorsements to new prospective healthcare clients may help you win contracts. The more letters of recommendation and testimonials you receive, the better.

Following completion of your work with every satisfied client, make it a habit to ask for a testimonial letter. You may give your client some guidance with points to include such as referencing to creative solutions, meeting deadlines, providing value, and the caliber of artists installed in the project. Use these testimonial letters as a tool to gain business. The more people brag about how competent and professional you are, the easier it will be to overcome barriers with prospects. Follow the logic. Since business people prefer to do business with people they trust and value, if you are a stranger, how can you get them to trust you? How will they know if you can deliver what they need? By showing testimonial letters from high profile clients (people they trust and value), this third party proof will lift many of their concerns.

Knowing that a top-notch company (similar to theirs) with a high socioeconomic clientele hired you and praised your performance, will undoubtedly register quite positively when a prospective client is considering you for a project. Sometimes, the executives reading the testimonials may actually know the people who wrote them. Your testimonials lend credibility, and in reality it is a small business world. Executives in similar fields have been known to exchange information and discuss vendors who have performed well. The point is to acquire many testimonials and use them often. Testimonials and referrals go hand in hand.

Another effective way to use endorsement letters is to post them on your website or use them in your ads. Effective testimonials should mention the impact your artwork had on the project, what skills you brought to the table, why the person recommends you, and the scope of the project. If certain obstacles or difficulties were overcome such as an unusual design solution or an out of the ordinary installation, these issues should be addressed. Copies of testimonial letters can also be framed and displayed in your place of business. Regularly ask for testimonial letters, show them to prospective clients, display them at your place of business, post them on your website, and consider using them in your ads. Testimonial letters carry weight and can help sway business in your direction.

It is easy to understand the impact testimonials can have on your business. The question is how do you get them. The answer is that you earn the right to ask for testimonials when you have performed well in all aspects of business. Satisfied clients will be happy to write them, but some may request direction about what to say about you. An effective testimonial letter will convey the benefits of selecting your company, show how obstacles were overcome and objectives were achieved, rate your abilities, and succinctly discuss how fears and risks evaporated during the client/company relationship. Art consultants should not be reluctant to ask satisfied clients for testimonial letters. It should be a routine business practice in completing all successful art programs.

Reasons to get endorsements letters:

1. Third party validations from high profile business people are powerful.
2. You can brag about your own abilities, but words from a satisfied client have more value and impact.
3. Prospective clients are interested in what other respected professionals have to say about you and your company.
4. Business people who read testimonial letters often know the person who wrote them, especially when they are in a similar business. High profile business people want to read what other business people have to say about your business practices and services.
5. Posting endorsement letters on your website will add credibility to your company.
6. Using excerpts from the letters of recommendations in your ads targeting specific audiences can be very effective.
7. Endorsements may help alleviate reservations prospective clients have in hiring you. When similar concerns are addressed in endorsement letters, risks and fears may become less objectionable.

Excerpts from client testimonials

"As an art consultant on a number of healthcare facilities design and interior projects, I have enjoyed working with Barbara. She always provided the projects with a large selection of art pieces and framing. As I am very much hands on in the art selection process, Barbara quickly learned my preferences and was prepared to provide a variety of options for my consideration. She respects one's choices and doesn't get offended if her suggestions are rejected. Barbara's finished product never ceases to impress me and gives a finishing touch worthy of recognition. Working with Barbara has been a very comfortable and enjoyable experience."

Sherwood Covill
Healthcare Facility Design Consultant
Scripps Health, San Diego

"Barbara is a very talented art consultant whose educational background and artistic expertise enhances her ability to provide quality service to designers and clients. With a Master of Art in Art Therapy, she is able to understand and integrate the image to the environment whether commercial, residential, or hospitality. Her knowledge and representation of various artists and the vast offering of poster art, allows her to pull from various resources to fulfill the desired image and feeling for the space. I value her opinion when selecting frames, mats, colors, and her keen eye when adjusting installation locations for my interior design projects. Her firm, Artrageous! complements her strengths with a team of installers and assistants who pay attention to detail, are very timely, and are courteous."

Nancy Suda
Principal Studio Suda
Certified Interior Designer

"Thank you so much for such an outstanding job on Studio 15's artwork. You decorated 5 stories of walls in a 275-unit project in downtown San Diego and I couldn't have dreamed of a better selection of prints. I only gave you a few ideas of color and what I was looking for and you just knew what to do. Even the architect, David Gonzales of Carrier Johnson Architects, wanted to meet you. He said, '…she knew what I was thinking and I never even met her… this woman is amazing.' Barbara, you were a dream to work with, and I hardly had to give you any direction; you were so professional and on schedule. You helped me achieve designing a beautiful building full of art and color even though it was an affordable housing project. From this project on I would be honored to have you on my team."

Yvonne DeCarlo
Office Manager
Affirmed Housing Group

"Art is the finishing touch to months of planning, design, and build out and is the element that makes the exclamation point. Working with Barbara and her team at Artrageous! was wonderful in every aspect: excellent resources for art, professional demeanor at every phase, and most importantly she listens to her customers. The end result was 2 state-of-the-art medical outpatient facilities with artwork that enhanced the design. The frame quality and installation were excellent. Patients have asked staff for the source of our artwork, and we proudly refer Barbara. I was so impressed, I ordered an original piece of art for my home and had the same professional advice and final product. Barbara and her team are the whole package."

Elaine Davis RN
Scripps Coastal Medical Center, Special Projects

"As a very satisfied client of Barbara Markoff and Artrageous! art consulting, I wanted to take a moment to share with you the appraisal of my working relationship with the team and the results of our collective efforts. I'm the Marketing Director of a fast growing and successful commercial bank in San Diego, California. Upon accepting the role, I relocated to San Diego from the Midwest. As such, I knew no one in town, and one of my responsibilities was to ensure the successful launch of our new office located in the Downtown district. When I met Barbara, I was immediately put at ease given her in-depth knowledge of her industry. Her approach enabled her to successfully walk me through the decision making process which ultimately led to wise choices in art selection. Barbara had the capacity and desire to help me in the selection which proved to the liking of our CEO and Chairman of the Board. With that level of personal service, you can imagine Barbara has been instrumental in helping me continue to open new business locations and enhance our existing facilities with artwork that is uniquely suited for our company."

Crystal Watkins
Senior Vice President
Director of Marketing and CRA Administration
Torrey Pines Bank

These excerpts are included to show a variety of client's comments with the intention of having you understand how powerful testimonials can be. As you grow your business and expand your client base, make an effort to obtain letters of recommendation. It is a "feel good" exercise; reading glowing and positive feedback from your clients is touching and rewarding. Receiving a testimonial gives you a sense of closure of a job well done. Remember your future sales may depend on the endorsements by others.

Chapter 22

Typical Sales Scenarios

The following are two fictitious scenarios which will demonstrate the step-by-step process of completing a corporate art program. The methods used are characteristic of the approach I take when working with corporate clients. Each art consultant has his/her own style and method of conducting business. It is my intention to guide you through these scenarios to help you understand my approach as outlined in this book.

Scenario A (new client and referral)

An upscale accounting firm has just moved into a building and calls you to schedule a meeting. Bill Edwards, the furniture representative supplying all of the new office furniture, referred the contact person, Beth Williams, to you. Beth explains the offices will require all new artwork and reframing of the executive's diplomas. She is unsure what style of artwork they want and is open to suggestions.

1. While still on the phone with Beth inquire about the size of the new location. Ask if the environment is contemporary or traditional. Inquire about the color palette of the décor and if they are considering fine art, poster art, or a combination of both.
2. Thank Beth for the opportunity to meet with her and ask the names and positions of the other decision makers.
3. Ask Beth what the time line for the project is and if they are planning an opening event.
4. Ask Beth for her contact information and set up the appointment at her convenience. Politely thank her again for the opportunity and end the call.
5. Call Bill Edwards and personally thank him for the referral. Ask Bill to send a floor plan for the facility since he is specifying the furniture.
6. Ask Bill to briefly discuss the new space and the type of furniture he is specifying. Find out about any additional pertinent information that may assist you with the project.
7. Thank Bill again and let him know you will keep him informed on how the referral progresses.
8. Begin to plan what artwork, catalogs, and binders to bring to the appointment. Focus on what style of fine art may be of interest to the decision makers. Select a variety of sources to bring with you since it is difficult to predict what the client will like.
9. 24 hours prior to the appointment confirm it with Beth.
10. Gather the artwork, catalogs, binders, and items from the materials list and arrive at the appointment 20 minutes early. Greet the receptionist, ask her name, and proceed to unload.
11. Meet with Beth and her two associates to discuss the art selection. Start the meeting by presenting a client list and company brochure. Exchange business cards. Listen to their likes and dislikes as you show the artwork and look at the binders and catalogs.

12. During the meeting, one of the decision makers mentions he really likes the San Diego photographic scenes and would like to do the entire office with landmark San Diego scenes. The other decision makers agree.

13. At this point, show all of the sources you have brought of San Diego photographic scenes and narrow down their selections to specific areas such as individual offices, conference rooms, reception area, break room, and hallways.

14. Briefly discuss framing styles and determine the exact number and image sizes of the pieces selected. Measure the diplomas that need reframing and write down the sizes. Ask to take photographs of the office and write down all pertinent information.

15. Thank the decision makers for the opportunity to be considered for the project. Conclude the meeting, load the artwork and materials, and return to your office.

16. While everything is fresh on your mind, prepare a proposal detailing the art selections and reframing of the diplomas. Send the proposal to Beth within 24 hours of the meeting via email.

17. Call or email Beth a day after the proposal was sent to confirm she received it. Inquire if she has any questions, and find out when a decision will be made.

18. You do not hear from Beth for two weeks during which time a decision should have been made. You wait patiently and decide to give Beth another week before you contact her again.

19. Beth emails to inform you the decision makers will be meeting with another art consultant soon and will let you know.

20. You wait to hear from Beth with the plan of contacting her if she has not contacted you within two weeks. About a week after your last communication with Beth, she calls stating you are the art consultant selected for the project because you had the largest selection of San Diego photographic images.

21. Beth wants to pay the 50% deposit by credit card immediately to ensure the order is completed in time for their opening party four weeks away.

22. You email Beth a credit card authorization form with the information needed to charge the deposit.

23. You order all of the artwork and framing materials. You make arrangements to pick up the diplomas. Once the artwork arrives you oversee the framing design and scheduling.

24. You write a personal thank you note to Bill Edwards telling him your company has been selected to provide the artwork and how appreciative you are for the referral.

25. One week prior to the deadline, you call Beth to schedule the installation. The type of installation was predetermined at the meeting. All framed pieces are inspected for quality control.

26. One day prior to the installation, you email Beth to confirm that payment will be ready for the balance due. The installation time is confirmed as well.

27. A delivery receipt is prepared.

28. The day of the installation, you and your crew arrive on time and install everything as planned. You walk the space with Beth to see if any additional pieces are needed and to get her feedback on the completed job.

29. Beth signs the delivery receipt and gives you a check for the balance due. She remarks how pleased she is with the outcome of the project.

30. With permission, you photograph the job with your digital camera.
31. You personally thank Beth and her associates for their business and conclude the installation.
32. You send Beth a personal thank you note and follow up with a phone call to see if she needs anything else.
33. Beth informs you one of the executives would like a San Diego photograph for his home. She supplies you with the contact information. You thank her and follow up on the new inquiry.
34. You attend the opening party and network effectively.
35. You call Beth within one week after installation and ask for a testimonial letter.
36. You add the company to your client list.

SCENARIO B (working with a repeat client)

A project manager that you have previously worked with emails you regarding an art program needed for a neighborhood outpatient health clinic. The email includes a scheduled meeting time, floor plan, and opening date of the facility. An attachment to the email provides visuals of the floor finishes, wallpaper, paint colors, and wood paneling. You have previously been hired to coordinate art programs for the same company including several similar facilities, which opened in the last two years. Therefore, you are familiar with their taste in art, budget concerns, and way of conducting business.

1. Email the project manager acknowledging the information sent and thank her for the opportunity. Review the artwork previously purchased by the client to refresh your memory about their selections. Go through your existing art inventory and select pieces for the project. Contact artists and art brokers to have additional pieces sent in for the presentation.
2. A day before the scheduled meeting, email the project manager to confirm the meeting.
3. Arrive at the meeting with an assistant to show a large selection of appropriate healthcare artwork. In addition, show artist binders and both fine art and poster art catalogs.
4. Discuss the primary areas where artwork should be placed. Mark these locations on the floor plan in pencil.
5. Determine the quantity of pieces needed and make preliminary selections from the artwork presented. Take detailed notes at the meeting.
6. Before concluding the meeting, schedule a second follow up meeting to review more art selections.
7. Gather more artwork to blend with the pieces selected from the first meeting. Choose three or four frame samples and check stock confirming availability.
8. At the second meeting, bring back the pieces selected from the first meeting along with another wide selection of artwork for review. Finalize all of the art selections and specify the art placement plan on the floor plan. Choose the frame and discuss the framing and installation details.
9. Prepare and submit a proposal via email to the project manager. Use your past knowledge of working with this company to help with pricing and specifications.
10. Because the project exceeds $40,000 and your company requires a 50% deposit on

orders exceeding $10,000, state the terms of payment to be a 50% deposit with the balance due NET 30 from the installation date.

11. Contact the project manager to confirm receipt of the proposal and inquire if she has any questions or concerns regarding the proposal.

12. You receive the purchase order. Review it to ensure its accuracy.

13. Generate an invoice for the 50% deposit and send it via email to the project manager.

14. Order all of the framing materials and artwork.

15. The deposit check arrives in the mail.

16. You receive the artwork and inspect it for quality control and to ensure the correct pieces were sent. Assign each piece a number corresponding to its placement on the floor plan. Send the framing design work orders through to the frame shop.

17. Schedule a tentative installation date and time.

18. The framing is completed. Inspect each piece for quality control and ensure the proper numbers have been assigned.

19. Reconfirm the date one week prior to the installation scheduled.

20. One day prior to the installation date reconfirm it again.

21. Arrive at the job site for the installation on time and unload the artwork. Place each piece in the location as per the floor plan. Before installing, review the art placement with the project manager to determine any changes from the original plan.

22. Work with the project manager to determine the height and positioning of the pieces.

23. Upon completion of the entire installation, request a walk through with the project manager. Complete the walk through and present the delivery receipt form for signature.

24. Ask permission to take digital photographs. Take photographs once permission has been granted.

25. Thank the project manager for the business, and make sure the job site is left clean of any debris caused by the installers.

26. Send an invoice with the delivery receipt form for the balance due.

27. Make a follow up phone call the next day to touch base and discuss the outcome of the project. If the project manager is unavailable, leave a voice message. Inquire if any additional pieces are needed.

28. Ask for a testimonial letter unless you already have a recent one from the project manager.

29. Send a written thank you note to the project manager.

30. Stop by the facility once it has opened for business. Drop off business cards to the receptionist and facility manager.

31. Attend the event celebrating the clinic's opening and network effectively.

32. Follow up on late payments by calling the accounting department.

33. Periodically touch base with the project manager to inquire about upcoming projects.

Chapter 23

Sample Forms

The following are sample forms of proposals, consignment agreements, delivery receipts, and other forms that will assist you in running your business smoothly. The profession of corporate art consultant requires many agreements and forms in order to protect your interests and assure that you are paid in a timely manner. Having experienced many bumps in the road along the way, I fully understand the need to develop forms and obtain signatures to alleviate repeat problems. The forms included are not intended to provide art consultants with every form needed, but to give you some direction. Each art consultant will obviously face different situations and institute their own methods of creating forms within their company.

Delivery Receipt Form

XYZ Company
234 Main Street
Anywhere, CA 90000

Delivery receipt

To:

New Medical Clinic
3333 New Medical Road
Anywhere, CA 90000

Purchase Order number _____
Number of pieces received _____
Received by (please print name) _____
Title _____ Date _____

The pieces received were all in excellent condition and satisfied the contract requirements.
Comments _____
_____
_____

Company representative _____

Delivery and Installation Request Form

- Delivery only
- Delivery & Installation
- Installation only – Art at Site

Date & Time of Installation _____

Installers Assigned _____

Job Name _____

Job Address _____

Contact Person _____

Phone Number _____

Company Representative _____

Number of Pieces _____

Confirmation of Installation: Spoke to _____

On this date _____

Job Site Information:

Number of Floors _____ Elevator Available _____

Number of Art Locations _____ Concrete Walls _____

Ladder Needed _____ Wallpaper _____

Other Instructions _____

List All Work Order Numbers _____

Artist Inquiries Form

Artwork Review Procedures for Possible Gallery
Representation By XYZ Art Consulting Services

1. Initial contact by artist may be made either by mail or email.
2. Please include a cover letter, biographical information, CD or photographs, NET pricing (the price you expect to receive for your art), and sizes available.
3. If you expect the information to be returned to you please include a self-addressed stamped envelope with the initial information packet. If the self-addressed stamped envelope is not included XYZ Art Consultation Services will not be responsible for returning the artist's packet.
4. Due to the large quantities of artist packets that XYZ Art Consulting Services receives, artists should understand that it may take up to 8 weeks to receive a response. Please do not call XYZ Art Consulting Services for immediate feedback.
5. If XYZ Art Consulting Services is interested in artist representation, our gallery director will contact you to discuss the artist relationship.
6. XYZ Art Consulting Services understands current copyright laws with respect to artwork.
7. Please email artist information to info@xyzacs.biz or mail to: 1234 Main Street, My Town, CA 66666 Attn: Gallery Director

Thank you for your interest in XYZ Art Consulting Services

Consignment Form

ABC Artist Studio
1234 Main Street
Anytown, CA 91111

Phone_____FAX_____Email _____

CONSIGNMENT AGREEMENT

The following art is hereby consigned to:

_____

_____

_____

For the period of_____to _____

QUANTITY	SIZE	TITLE/DESCRIPTION	PRICE

Upon expiration of the consignment period the artwork shall be returned upon request to the artist, or paid in full. The consignee agrees to insure the artwork at all times. Any defects must be noted in writing at the time the artwork is accepted on consignment and noted on this form. Artwork lost, stolen, or damaged shall be purchased by the consignee without protest as the stated value. Any request by the artist to have artwork returned prior to the agreed return date will be met with no opposition. The consignee shall not reproduce the art in any form without prior authorization from the artist.

ARTIST	CONSIGNEE	DATE
_____	_____	_____

Art on Approval

XYZ Company
55 MAIN STREET
ANYTOWN, NY 55555

NAME_____

ADDRESS_____

PHONE_____Agreement for _____days

DATE_____

Artist/Title	Quantity	Retail	Net

Consigned artwork shall be insured by the borrower and returned in good condition within the agreed time period. Borrower agrees to pay for any artwork with marks, damage, tears, or that has been lost or stolen. Borrower agrees to pay all attorney fees incurred by lender in enforcing this agreement. All artwork sold shall be invoiced immediately. All artwork shall be returned upon request and borrower shall pay for shipping of artwork back to XYZ Company.

Client signature/date   Company Representative

_____   _____

May 14, 2009

XYZ Healthcare Company
1234 Healthcare Court
Main Town, CA 90000
222-000-8000 Voice
222-000-8001 Fax

Proposal

Overview of project:

Artrageous!, an art and framing company established in 1981, will provide the art program for XYZ Healthcare's new West Care clinic opening June 22, 2009. Nature themed artwork has been selected to help welcome both patients and visitors and staff members. 42 framed pieces with identifying name plates will be placed in the waiting rooms and corridors. The purpose of this project is to incorporate a specialized art program that will create an uplifting environment conducive to healing for all West Care patients.

Scope of work:
• Review blueprints to determine quantity of pieces and art placement
• Selection of artwork based on size, subject matter, and price
• Presentations and meetings with XYZ Healthcare Company architect, Jim Wong, project manager
• Provide visuals of each piece of artwork approved for project
• Design and execution of all picture framing required
• Provide name tags for each piece of artwork selected
• Preparation of proposals including revisions to meet budget concerns
• Delivery of artwork to job site
• Assisting in art place placement during installation

Reimbursables:
Artwork specified

Piece #	Art description	Approximate framed size	Price
FIRST FLOOR WAITING ROOM, NORTH SIDE			
1	Smith - Beach Scene 1	32 x 42	750.00
2	Smith - Beach Scene 2	32 x 42	750.00
3	Smith - Beach Scene 3	32 x 42	750.00
4	Smith - Beach Scene 4	32 x 42	750.00
5	Smith - Beach Scene 5	32 x 42	750.00
FIRST FLOOR WAITING ROOM, WEST SIDE			
6	Smith - Garden 1	32 x 41	650.64
7	Smith - Garden 2	38 x 35	1066.72
8	Smith - Garden 3	38 x 35	1066.72

| 9 | Smith - Garden 4 | 44 x 29 | 1066.72 |

FIRST FLOOR WAITING ROOM, SOUTH SIDE

10	Moore - Nature Way 1	44 x 54	1081.92
11	Moore - Nature Way 2	44 x 54	1081.92
12	Moore - Nature Way 3	44 x 34	921.92
13	Moore - Nature Way 4	44 x 34	921.92

FIRST FLOOR WAITING ROOM, EAST SIDE

14	Alan - Leaves	44 x 54	961.92
15	Alan - Stones	44 x 36	750.00
16	Alan - Creek	36 x 49	865.36
17	Alan - Valley	30 x 39	925.92
18	Alan - Lagoon	34 x 44	750.00

FIRST FLOOR, CORRIDOR 1272

19	Beck - Floral A	29 x 26	504.10
20	Beck - Floral B	29 x 26	504.10
21	Beck - Floral C	29 x 26	504.10

FIRST FLOOR, CORRIDOR 1277

| 22 | Strong - Koi I | 20 x 20 | 375.88 |
| 23 | Strong - Koi II | 20 x 20 | 375.88 |

FIRST FLOOR, CORRIDOR 10

24	Roy - Morning	37 x 30	650.65
25	Roy - Dusk	37 x 30	650.65
26	Dell - Lakeside	37 X 34	650.65
27	Dell - Sunsong	34 x 45	750.00
28	Dell - Pines	44 x 54	1081.92

PEDIATRICS

29	Frank - Doves	30 x 40	800.00
30	Frank - Shells	43 x 39	861.34
31	poster (to be determined)	32 x 40	195.00
32	client provided piece	16 x 20	n/c
33	poster (to be determined)	32 x 40	195.00
34	client provided piece	16 x 20	n/c
35	poster (to be determined)	32 x 40	195.00

LARGE WALL ACROSS FROM EXAM ROOM 2

36	Richal - Blooms	46 x 46	1081.92
37	Norris - Calm Creek	41 x 49	865.36
38	Norris - River Bed	43 x 38	627.28

HALLWAY 1450

39	Ruth - Dogwoods	33 x 41	650.64
40	Ruth - Spring Now	30 x 41	650.64
41	Ruth - Evergreens	24 x 24	438.32

EMPLOYEE LOUNGE

42	poster (to be determined)	32 x 40	195.00

Security hardware @ $5.00 x 42	210.00
Security wrench	7.50
Typesetting, printing, identification plates @ 10.00 each	420.00
Subtotal	30,802.61
Sales Tax	2,695.23

Nontaxable items:

Art placement services billed @ $60.00 per hour	
4 hours estimated (additional hours to be billed separately)	240.00
Site presentations 7 hours @ $60.00 per hour	420.00
Courier services	20.00
Shipping charges	200.00
Overtime charges to rush order, 16 hours @ $90.00 per hour	1440.25
Trip charge	25.00
Total	$35,842.84

Job specifications:

All artwork double matted with archival paper mats, glazed with ultra violet filtering clear glass. Oversize pieces glazed with regular acrylic. Frame is 2" cherry colored wood on regular size pieces and 4" cherry colored frame on oversize pieces.

Price includes delivery to job site in one scheduled delivery. Return trips will be billed at $25.00 if work cannot be received due to construction problems.

Terms are 50% deposit and balance due NET 30 from date of delivery

August 4, 2009

Ocean Medical Hospital
Beth Peters
Project Manager
Facilities Design & Construction
12345 Ocean Avenue
Ocean, CA 92000

Quotation

Location	Item	Price
Floor One	30 framed posters @ $225.00 each	6550.00
Floor Two	50 framed posters @ $225.00 each	11,250.00
Floor Three	46 framed posters @ $225.00 each	10,350.00
Floor Four	39 framed posters @ $225.00 each	8775.00
Floor Five	41 framed posters @ $225.00 each	9225.00
Floor Six	50 framed posters @ $225.00 each	11,250.00
Floor Seven	40 framed posters @ $225.00 each	9000.00
Floor Eight	40 framed posters @ $225.00 each	9000.00
	Subtotal	75,400.00
	Sales Tax	6,597.50
	Total	$81,997.50

Installation to be billed separately
Specifications: 3" amber colored wood frame, double matted with archival mats,
glazed with conservation clear glass, security hardware, all pieces sized inside dimensions
between 24 x 36 and 32 x 40
Terms: 50% deposit, balance net 30 from installation date
Turnaround time approximately 4 weeks from receipt of purchase order and deposit check

Chapter 24

Final Thoughts

In a new profession such as art consultation, little published reference material exists to navigate individuals through the process of developing and implementing an art program. Art production distinguishes man from all other living creatures and bonds him to nature. Art reflects a conscious act of interpreting and stating interactions characteristic of the living existence of man. The profound impact artwork may have in places where people tend to gather cannot be underestimated. Consequently, art consultants have an immense responsibility in selecting artwork appropriate for a wide range of audiences in numerous settings. It is not an easy task.

By writing this book, my intention is to share my years of experience as a corporate art consultant so that design professionals may benefit from these experiences. I did not set out to become a corporate art consultant; my business guided me in that particular direction. The journey has been personally satisfying and at times quite fun. It is a labor intensive and demanding profession not for individuals easily discouraged. In order to succeed as a corporate art consultant, a multitude of skills are necessary. I hope this book will prove to be a beneficial resource for all those interested in becoming a corporate art consultant.

I would like to personally thank my husband, Rob Markoff, who brought me into the framing industry in 1982 when I was laid off from my job as an art therapist. He taught me "everything I know about picture framing." After 10 years of working and framing for others, Rob started his own picture framing business in 1981. The rest is history. I thank him for his support and encouragement in completing this book. I also want to thank our daughter, Rachel, who is a shining light in my life.

A deep and sincere thank you goes to Marc Bluestone, who suggested I write an article for Picture Framing Magazine on the subject of art consultation. Had it not been for Marc, I would not have started writing. I would also like to thank Laurie Bluestone for her encouragement and continued support. She is one of my best cheerleaders, and she too worked as a corporate art consultant lending her ear along the way.

Patrick Sarver, editor of Picture Framing Magazine, has been instrumental in encouraging me to write about the profession of corporate art consultation. I want to thank him for editing my articles and giving me the opportunity to write for Picture Framing Magazine. I would also like to personally thank Debbie Salmon and Bruce Gherman who hired me to teach classes on art consultation and networking at The West Coast Art & Frame Show. Teaching classes on these subjects helped me organize my thoughts and take the time to outline each aspect of the process I go through in selling an art program.

I would like to acknowledge Todd Holley and Ben Price who run Entransa, the first networking group I joined in San Diego. Being part of Entransa has been a life changing experience for me and my business, and I feel very fortunate to have been a part of this dynamic group. Through Entransa, I learned about information sharing, and I met wonderful, motivated individuals. In addition, I would like to thank Patty Wise, my first business networking friend, who taught me the ropes and the importance of connecting with the right people.

I extend a special thanks to my sister, Carol Burkhart, for her unwavering support and confidence in my abilities. She is a constant source of inspiration and finds humor in unexpected places. Thank you also to my brothers, Alan Greenberg and Elliot Greenberg, for reading my articles early on and encouraging me to continue writing business articles. I would also like to thank my dear friend, Jill Wlos, for her support and wisdom in this endeavor. Jill read all of my articles leading up to this book, and her positive outlook and perspective mean the world to me.

It is my hope that this book will serve as a useful tool to art consultants, gallery owners, picture framers, interior designers, artists, design professionals, and all those thinking about entering the profession. If this book sparks your interest, I also offer coaching to individuals who want to enter the profession. My business email is Barbara@theartconsultant.biz. I look forward to hearing from you.

References

Fine Art and Poster Art Publishing Companies:

Artaissance	888-351-0169	www.artthatfits.com
Bentley Publishing Group	800-227-1666	www.bentleypublishinggroup.com
Bruce McGaw Graphics	800-221-4814	www.brucemcgaw.com
Bruce Teleky	800-835-3539	www.teleky.com
Canadian Art Prints	800-663-1166	www.canadianartprints.com
Deljou Art Group	800-237-4638	www.deljouartgroup.com
Dry Brush Graphics	800-228-0928	www.drybrushgraphics.com
Editions Limited	800-228-0928	www.editionslimited.com
Gango Editions	800-852-3662	www.gangoeditions.com
Grand Image	800-900-3551	www.grandimage.com
Haddad's Fine Arts	800-942-3323	www.haddadsfinearts.com
Image Conscious	800-532-2333	www.imageconscious.com
Mercurius Art Publishing	212-255-3434	www.mapartpublishing.com
New Era Publishing	888-445-3236	www.newerahd.com
New York Society Publishing Group	800-677-6947	www.nygs.com
Pecheur Images	866-684-6390	www.plisson.com
Phoenix Art Group	800-842-5487	www.phxartgroup.com
Poems Art Publishing	888-447-6367	www.poemsart.com
Posters International	800-363-2787	www.postersinternational.net
Rosensteils's Fine Art Publishers (International)	+44(0)20 7352 3551	www.felixr.com
Third and Wall	877-326-3925	www.thirdandwall.com
Top Art	800-253-0102	www.topart.net
Wild Apple Graphics	800-756-8359	www.wildapple.com
Winn Devon	800-663-1166	www.winndevon.com
World Art Group	804-213-0600	www.oldworldprintsltd.com

Picture Frame Moulding Vendors

To find an up-to-date list of leading moulding vendors, visit www.pictureframingmagazine.com and click on "Buyers Guide."

Free online sources:

"Picture of Health, Handbook for Healthcare Art." By Henry Domke, M.D.
To find it online, this is the URL:
www.henrydomke.com/PictureOfHealth.pdf

Jeffrey Gitomer's "Sales Caffeine "
Subscribe to this ezine at: www.gitomer.com

About the author:

Barbara Markoff is a businesswoman, writer, devoted mother, teacher, and art consultant. A pioneer in the field of art sales to business clients, she has provided art programs for over 400 corporate clients. In addition to teaching classes on the topics of business networking and corporate art sales, Barbara coaches individuals interested in entering the profession. Before becoming a corporate art consultant Barbara worked as an art therapist with abused adolescent girls. She and her husband, Rob, run Artrageous!, a successful art and framing company in San Diego, California. Barbara resides in Encinitas, a beach community north of San Diego with Rob.